The
Secret Lives
of
Elves & Faeries

The
Secret Lives
of
Elves & Faeries

From the Private Journal
of
THE REV. ROBERT KIRK

Being the Newly Discovered Story of the
Rev. ROBERT KIRK, minister of Aberfoyle in
Scotland, as recorded by himself after a period
spent in the realm of Faery, including a
description of the beings encountered there, as
told for his son, Colin, before he vanished from
the sight of men, into that place of which he had
written and to which his heart rightly belonged.

by
JOHN MATTHEWS

Illustrations by George Sharp & Rob McCaig

To RJS for the visions of Faery. JM

Element
An Imprint of HarperCollins*Publishers*
77–85 Fulham Palace Road
Hammersmith, London W6 8JB

The website address is: www.thorsonselement.com

element ™ and *Element* are trademarks of
HarperCollins*Publishers* Ltd

First published in the US by Element 2005

First published in Great Britain in 2005 by
Godsfield Press, a division of Octopus Publishing Group Ltd
2–4 Heron Quays, London E14 4JP

1 3 5 7 9 10 8 6 4 2

A catalogue record of this book is available from the British Library

ISBN 0 00 720071 4

Printed and bound in China by Toppan

Contents

THE FAIRY MINISTER

He heard, he saw, he knew too well
The secrets of your fairy clan;
You stole him from the haunted dell,
Who never more was seen of man,
Now far from heaven, and safe from hell,
Unknown of earth, he wanders free.
Would that he might return and tell
Of his mysterious company!

And half I envy him who now,
Clothed in her court's enchanted green,
By moonlit loch or mountain's brow
Is chaplain to the Fairy Queen.

Andrew Lang

Introduction:
The Discovery of
the Manuscript

With the passage of time, there are fewer and fewer opportunities to record folklore from those who actually remember it. Yet the documents that have survived, mostly taken down by collectors in the 18th and 19th centuries, hold within them important clues to the beliefs and traditions of people everywhere that would otherwise have been forgotten.

The term 'folklore' dates from the end of the 19th century, when interest in such matters was actually lessening; but few would deny that folklore serves as a last strand connecting us with a time now lost for ever. It is the repository of the beliefs that kept our ancestors in touch with an even older time, when gods walked the earth and the people of Faery were abroad under the moon.

One of the most important of these documents is a work known as *The Secret Commonwealth of Elves, Fauns and Faeries*, written by a Scots minister named Robert Kirk between 1688 and 1692. Kirk's detailed accounts of the Faery races have become an essential part of Faery lore and tradition and have been edited before. But the full story of how they came to be written has never been told, for the simple reason that it has remained unknown until this moment, the assumption always being that Kirk assembled his book from local lore and traditions. The true source is somewhat other, and completely astonishing, as can now be told.

My own involvement in all this began when I learned, quite by chance, of an elderly woman – a Mrs Jean Seldy – living in a remote village in Scotland who was said to possess a fascinating collection of materials relating to the folklore of the area, left to her by her great-grandmother, Mrs Greentye of Balquhidder. I immediately determined to investigate further and made my way north.

Mrs Seldy was a bright-eyed and birdlike woman with white hair framing a lined but alert face. She welcomed me kindly and we partook of the ritual of tea and cake before doing anything else. It was only after some time that she mentioned the bequest from her great-grandmother. For such a collection to have remained unknown was a rare thing, so when Mrs Seldy finally indicated the old, iron-bound trunk standing in one corner of her sitting room and invited me to open it, I was obviously excited.

I sifted quickly though a number of manuscripts, letters and notes, and realized at once that there was a good deal of interest here. Then, towards the bottom of the trunk, I came upon a bundle of papers, loosely tied in faded ribbon, that I could see from the writing alone belonged to an earlier period than the rest. As soon as I saw the inscription on the cover a shiver ran through me. I knew that I had discovered something of great importance – though just how important was not clear until later.

THE SECRET LIVES OF ELVES & FAERIES
The Private Journal of the Rev. ROBERT
KIRK, minister of Aberfoyle in Scotland,
as recorded by himself during a period spent
in the realm of Faery
and including a description of the beings
encountered there.
1692.

I knew, of course, of the writings of Robert Kirk, but to come across what was evidently a manuscript copy from this early date was remarkable. Hitherto the book had been known only in a transcript made for Kirk's son in 1693 and two copies, both deriving from this, which were now in the National Library of Scotland and Edinburgh University

Library. As I looked through the pages I realized that this was not simply a manuscript copy but very possibly the manuscript written by Robert Kirk himself – or at least one so close to the original that it made little difference. It was also clear that this was a much longer version than any of those hitherto known.

On the day in question, only Mrs Seldy's offer of more tea recalled me to myself. It was not until later, having obtained her permission – generously given – to remove the papers for further study, that I finally came to understand what I had stumbled upon.

In order to measure the importance of the discovery it is necessary to say a few words about the Reverend Robert Kirk's life and work. Other matters, which include some highly speculative ideas concerning his death, must also be considered, especially in the light of evidence contained in the new manuscript. However, for reasons that will become clear, I shall postpone this until the end of the book.

Robert Kirk was born in 1644, the seventh son of James and Mary, in the parish of Aberfoyle in Perthshire, Scotland. His father was minister of the parish from 1639 until his early death in 1658. Kirk himself grew up among the wild and beautiful Highland landscape, and spent many hours on or around the famous 'faery hill' at Aberfoyle – a site that was to play such an important part in his later life. Receiving a bursary to attend Edinburgh University, Kirk graduated with an MA in 1661 and went from there to serve in the parish of Balquhidder, where he remained until 1688. During this time he married Isobel Campbell, the daughter of Sir Colin Campbell of Mochaster. Their only son, Colin, to whom the manuscript is addressed, later followed his grandfather's profession, that of notary, in Edinburgh. Isobel Kirk died suddenly in 1680 and it is said that Kirk himself carved the inscription for her tombstone. Shortly afterwards, he moved to his father's old parish of Aberfoyle and took up the post of minister, which he held until his own death in 1692, aged forty-eight.

Kirk's literary aspirations prompted him to undertake a number of tasks, including the translation and publication of the Psalter in Gaelic metrical verse. But it was his interest in the folklore of the local people and in particular that relating to the Faery races that occupied his every spare moment. He began making notes and taking down verbatim accounts from his parishioners while he was still in Balquhidder and several notebooks are still extant in the collection of Edinburgh University Library (MS La.III.545).

Subsequent editions of the work all appear to have been heavily edited. It would seem that the editors – one of whom may have been no lesser person than Samuel Pepys – deliberately excised every one of Kirk's personal references and reflections, together with his account of entering the Faery howe, leaving only the bare bones of his observations behind. Kirk himself comments (see page 120) that many people would regard his work as the ravings of an aberrant mind, and this seems to have been the case. Whoever finally brought his book into print in the form we know it today (we are not certain who this was) made sure that it lacked anything that might be considered tainted with madness or imagination, retaining only those materials that were considered valuable to collectors of Highland folklore. Those with expertise in the field who could read between the lines may well have already suspected that Kirk's work contained more than a simple minister with an interest in local lore could easily have discovered, but few would have believed the extraordinary details found in this full account.

Just how Mrs Greentye of Balquhidder came into possession of the version of Kirk's book edited here remains a mystery. Presumably the manuscript must have been given (or lent?) to a relative in Kirk's old parish, where it remained, forgotten, after his death. A comparison of the writing with that in Kirk's notebooks makes it virtually certain to be the original text, written by Kirk himself shortly before his death.

The versions that were previously known remain fascinating documents in their own right, but it is to Kirk's own words that we turn here. I can only speculate that the later editions were edited by those who disbelieved Kirk's account of his journey to Faery and wished to suppress the sensational details in order to spare the sensibilities of devout Christian readers, or that Kirk's own family removed all references to the actual source of his information for similar reasons. With the restoration of these missing pages we can once again read Robert Kirk's work in its entirety. I have added subheadings to the text throughout to make it more readable and to assist those seeking specific paragraphs. Other than this, the manuscript is word for word as Robert Kirk left it in 1692. And what an astonishing work it is. Whether or not readers believe his statements regarding his visits to the realm of Faery remains a matter of personal choice. That Kirk himself believed them to be true is without doubt.

A Note on the Illustrations

Scattered haphazardly throughout the manuscript of *The Secret Lives of Elves & Faeries* are a number of illustrations and sketches, some in colour and others in pencil. Many were severely damaged and difficult to decipher, but the fact that they appear to have been made by the Reverend Kirk himself – almost like photographs of Faery – makes them a hugely important part of the collection. When the time came for this book to be published, I wanted very much to include them, but their condition made them difficult or impossible to reproduce (other than the one included here on page 25, which is just clear enough to suggest a glimpse of the landscape of Faery). In the end I simply gave the pictures into the hands of two very talented artists, George Sharpe and Rob McCaig, who made the versions of them which now grace this volume. They are not Kirk's originals, but they capture the feeling of these in a way that is truly remarkable.

JOHN MATTHEWS
OXFORD, 2004

The
Secret Lives
of
Elves & Faeries

For now we see through a glass, darkly;
but then face to face.

1 CORINTHIANS 13.12

The Faery Howe

I believe that it was no accident that I came to the gates of the Faery realm.

Ever since I was a child I had played around and upon the great Faery howe, or mound, which lay but a small way from the church of grey stones from which my father dispensed the teachings of the faith, and where I in my turn was so to do some years later. Among the common folk of Aberfoyle, and elsewhere throughout the Gaelic lands, there were tales told of the howe, that strange lights had been seen above it, and that figures of an unearthly kind had been observed moving about the area around it. I myself believe that I once saw some such creature while still a child, though the memory of it is dim now. It was much to my father's dismay that such tales held a powerful fascination for me, and he was ever concerned to dissuade me from this interest in favour of a deeper love of Our Lord's ways. Yet it has long been my belief that the old ways of this ancient land, which seem part of the very stones themselves, offer no contradiction to the teachings of the Lord God, but are rather a confirmation of the wondrous diversity and divine order of His creation, and therefore I remained obdurate despite my father's stern warnings against the heathenish beliefs of the people.

• • •

So for some time I have gathered all that I can find and recorded
in notebooks many tales concerning the Faery races, the belief in
the second sight and the visionary skills of seership. But it is not
only the words of the common people that I wish to record, but
rather my own observations of the people who are variously called
Faery, the Sidhe, the Sluagh Maith or Good Folk, Lusbartan, the
People of Peace, Caiben, etc., etc. How I was able to explore the
realm and history of that people, and of the wonders I have seen, I
shall now tell.

The Magic Doorway

It was on a fair evening in the month of May that I wandered
close by that piece of earth known to all as the Faery howe. A
full round moon being but lately risen, the
land was bathed in pearly light, and by
its glow my footsteps were led, as so often
before, to the foot of the mound. Then it
was that suddenly I heard a strange,
wild music, the source of which was
unknown to me. As I pressed forward
around the side of the mound, I saw
light, bright as day, issuing from it,
such as might come from any door left
ajar on a warm night after dark. So bright was
this light, and so strong the pull of the music in my ears, that I

went forward without hesitation, and found myself looking into the howe itself.

Yet here was no earthen door, or rough dark place, but instead a shapely carven doorframe of mortared stone, and beyond it a passageway, flagged and straight, leading downwards. It was from the depths of this place that the bright, bold light and sound of harps and pipes and other instruments strange to my ears issued forth into the night. Also I smelled a wondrous scent, as of roses or other flowers that blossom in the summer. As I looked within, there came to my mind the stern warnings of my father, how the beings spoken of by the poor folk were wicked and filled with hateful spite towards humankind, and that the very fact of their living beneath the ground was clear enough indication of their unwholesome origins. But I thought also of the stories imparted to me by the good folk of Aberfoyle and elsewhere, which painted another kind of picture. But most of all I was pricked forward by a great and abiding curiosity to see what lay within the howe.

• • •

Therefore I took a step across the threshold, and then another upon the white stones of the passage, and then a third and so on, until I had walked further into the mound than its actual breadth, but always downwards, by a gentle slope. Then suddenly, as I was mindful of turning back, I emerged into a place of such wonder that even now I am scarcely able to describe it without trembling.

The Faery Dance

What lay before me was a cavern, but of such vast proportions that one might have set the whole village of Aberfoyle, and much of the land around, within it. It was most brightly lit, though by what means I could not tell, other than that it seemed the very walls of the place gave forth light. And there, before my astonished sight, I had my first glimpse of the people of that place. For in the midst of the great cavern danced a huge rout of folk, many hundred I believe, and of many different sizes and shapes. Tall and stately beings, greater in height than any living man or woman, and very bright and noble-seeming, turned gracefully among smaller, darker, stranger beings seemingly clad in garments made of tree bark or skins of animals. Their dancing was graceful and fine, and as ordered as one might see in a drawing room of Edinburgh city itself. But these were no mortal dancers but other, strange and wondrous folk. I saw there beings who seemed more like trees than humankind, yet who danced just as lightly; while others were short and squat of form, with gnarled and weathered faces, whose steps, though firmer than those of their companions, were no less elegant for all that. Indeed, in all my life I never saw a more bright and joyful company, for all their strangeness and variety of form.

• • •

And there to one side were the musicians who made such harmonious, sweet melody as ever I have heard: fiddlers, harpers, pipers and more played on instruments of strange and marvellous shape, such as made me long to dance also – though I cut a poor figure when it comes to such things.

The King and Queen

Then as I stood thus, amazed and wondering, there came towards me one of the dancers, a tall and bright figure that seemed half transparent, and held out a hand to me to come and join them. Nor could I resist, but despite my clumsiness, went willingly to join in the dance. And now I found a wonderful thing: that I too was able to foot it with the best, and spin and caper and whirl as well as any of that marvellous rout! And thus I danced, for how long I cannot say, until at last the music ceased and the dancers came to rest. Many there were who looked at me, not unkindly, but with a certain curiosity I thought.

• • •

Then it was that the being who had first brought me into the dance, or one so like it as to be an exact simulacrum, beckoned me to come and stand before two thrones, made of crystal I think, that stood to one side of the dancing round. There were seated two beings of such stately and glorious beauty that neither pen nor brush can do justice to them. It came to my mind that if these were people of the Faery race, and if as such they were less in every way than angels, then the beauty of angels must be beyond mortal sight and too great a thing to bear. But that day I was able to look upon them, and saw that they smiled and were merry, as well as solemn and terrible in their beauty.

One I deemed male and the other female, and thus I thought them King and Queen of that place. The Queen it was who bent a gracious look upon me and spoke in a voice so filled with music that it seemed to me I heard bells chime within it, or flutes blowing sweet melodies.

'Welcome, Robert Kirk,' she said. 'Long have you studied our ways and long have we watched you pass about your brief flock of days. Therefore it seemed good to us that we should meet and that you should learn more of us, for there have been many misreportings made in your world, and we would see this ended.'

Though I struggled mightily to reply in as fair a speech as possible, I fear that I but mumbled and stammered and faltered in my amazement at hearing this. If so, neither the King nor the Queen seemed offended, but instead summoned one from among the ranks of those who stood by. This being was almost as fair in my eyes as the Queen, but perhaps a little less in stature – though I had still to crane my neck to look into his face. (I say his, though in truth I was often confounded as to the sex of those to whom I spoke – often at length – for their voices were ever light and musical, and their forms tall and willowy and draped in garments that made them seem more graceful than any human.)

The Queen spoke to this being in a language that remains unknown to me. So subtle and complex were the sounds that,

though I have since studied long and hard to master it, my clumsy tongue could not find any means to shape them. My hosts, however, seemed to find no difficulty in addressing me, and were able to make even the rough tones of my language sound like a song. Indeed, it is my belief that wherever the Faery races are found, they will always speak in the tongue of that place, and dress in the manner of the people when they encounter them, the better to pass unseen in the Lands Above. Whether this makes them skilful linguists or simply better mimics, I know not. Perhaps it is we who hear them in the tongue of our own place – who can say?

The Faery being who had been summoned forth now spoke to me. 'I am Keenaymikilhighnapa,' he said. (Thus as near as possible I record it, for after this I was permitted to speak of this being as Kee.) 'It is my task to show you our realm and to answer any questions that you might have, and to enable you to record in your writing whatsoever is permitted of our kind.'

I know that I stumbled out some words of thanks, of wonder and amazement at this singular honour, and that they were kindly received. And so I found myself walking through the great cavern by the side of my guide, and learning from him certain things that I must be aware of if I was to accomplish the task I had been set. Firstly I was told that there were certain times of the moon when I could enter the howe, and that I had free passage in and out, always on the understanding that I brought nothing with me other than

my writing tools, brushes and paints, and that in
turn I took nothing out of the Faery realm
(this last was said with great solemnity,
and I was given also to understand that if
I broke this prohibition the doors to the
otherworldly realm would be closed to me
for ever after). Also, it was made known
to me that while I sojourned in the Faery
realm no time, as I knew it, would pass in
the outer world. Thus I would be able to
remain therein as long as I wished and
return home no more than a moment after
I had departed. That a day might come
when I no longer wished to return was a
matter not then raised, nor shall I refer to it again
until the proper time. Suffice it to say that on that first
occasion I spent a happy hour, as we would measure it, in the
company of the being I would henceforward know as Kee, and
afterwards returned home in a state of great elation, to find that,
indeed, no time had passed in this world we call home. How this
may be remains unknown to me, but perchance it accounts for the
great age attained by the Faery races. For what is to them but a
blink of an eye may be accounted many hours or days to us.

Exploring the Lands Beneath

Thus began my visits to the enchanted Lands Beneath, as I swiftly learned to call them. I soon found that the cavern was no more than a tiny piece of the Faery realms. Beyond it lay a vast land, under a great sky that was lit with sun, moon and stars like to our own, but brighter, closer it seemed, and still somehow beneath the earth above. So too I came to know and understand the different natures of the several races that dwelled beneath, and even something – so much as they knew – of their history and origins. This I have set forth below, in the best order that I can, to illuminate the unearthly realms as best I may. My few poor sketches and paintings are placed here as a visual record of what I saw – though I fear it is beyond the skills of even the greatest of artists (which I am assuredly not) to replicate all that I saw as I wandered on Faery ways.

• • •

After a time, as I grew accustomed to the subtle colours and shades of that place, I began to see how these immortal beings moved in our world also. Often then as I went about my everyday pursuits I caught shy glimpses of one of the Faery race, walking almost in the steps of a clumsy human being, laughing, jesting or carrying out some secret task of which I knew nothing.

But ever, ever, my knowledge grew and with it an increasing sense of wonder and delight. The peoples of the otherworlds,

whatever their origins, were no evil emanation of the Devil, but rather a grand, fierce, gentle, romantic, brotherly, wise and ancient folk from whom, if truth be told, we may yet learn much. It is in this spirit that I write these words this sixteenth day of October, sixteen hundred and eighty-eight, as God is my judge, Rob't Kirk of the parish of Aberfoyle in the country of Scotland.

Exploring the Faery Realm

In the weeks and then months that followed, I made my way to the great howe and, knocking as I had been told, gained entry there. Always, as though they were already aware of my presence even before I had announced myself, I found Kee awaiting me, ever ready to guide me into some new part of the Lands Beneath so that I might explore them and learn of those who dwelled there. My guide was ever courteous and in general willing to answer whatsoever questions I asked of him. Thus over time I began to know about the nature of the different races that lived below, how they formed themselves into tribes that constitute a kind of commonwealth of elves and others. Despite my wanderings, I believe that I have still not encountered every kind that dwell there, but such as I have met with I will try to describe – always aware that I am but a momentary traveller in the vastness and ancientness of the Lands Beneath. Often, indeed, have I brought to mind the words of our great poet Dunbar:

> Me thought the place all bright with lamps was lit,
> And therein entered many a lusty wight:
> Some young, some old, in sundry wise arrayed;
> Some sang, some danced, on instruments some played,
> Some made disport with hearts both glad and light.
>
> Then thought I thus: this is a mighty Faery,
> Or else my wit right wondrously doth vary.
> This seems to be a goodly company;
> And if it be but friendly fantasy,
> Defend me, Jesu and His mother, Mary.

A Proud People

The Sidhe are the largest of these races, and are, I believe, midway in nature between men and angels (as were daemons once thought to be). They are intelligent, studious, and possessed of light, changeable bodies (like those called astral) somewhat of the nature of a condensed cloud, and best seen in twilight. These bodies enable them to appear or disappear at pleasure. Also they are most beautiful to look upon, both the males and the females, being extremely tall and stately, with hair that seems most like webs of spider-silk, often of such length that it falls below the waist.

• • •

Some have bodies so thin and delicate that they are
fed only by drinking a kind of fine, spiritous
liquor like pure air; others feed on the
substance of corn that grows on the surface of
the earth, and which they steal away,
unseen, preying on the grain as do crows and
mice. Others, of a more substantial kind, are
known as Brownies. These are small in
stature, and stocky, with high domed
foreheads from which the hair recedes
(though this is no sign of age, but rather a
feature of the species). These I have
observed to bake bread, boil stews and take
vegetables from the earth. Many of them
are known to enter human homes, though
only when everyone is at rest. There, they set
kitchens in order, cleansing all the vessels in
return for a few scraps from the table. While
we have plenty, they often experience
scarcity in their homes, since they are not
given to catching as much prey as they might
require. Their robberies notwithstanding,
they sometimes cause great ricks of corn to
'bleed', as they call it (meaning, in truth, to
steal from the centre of the rick; how was never
revealed to me). On occasion they take so much as to cause great

distress to the farmers, who none the less make do with it, mostly to avoid reprisals by these small folk, whom they both fear and respect. It should also be said that, despite this seeming thievery, the Faery people often give back as much or more than they take, for they are a proud people, and I will say, too, that without their presence the world would be a poorer place in many ways.

● ● ●

In addition to the Sidhe, I have met with the Sprigguns, the Phenoderee, the Sylvans and the Kobbold among others, each of which is a wholly separate tribe or race among the entire commonwealth. Of these I intend to speak further, as I describe my wanderings in the Lands Beneath in more detail.

Faery Dwellings

After my first visit, I was made welcome in a number of Faery dwellings. Many are as old as the world itself, for the earth is full of cavities and holes, and in these the Faery races make their homes – next, as it were, to humankind, but separated from us by the greatest distance of kind. Once, I was informed, they too lived above ground, and tilled the earth, and the print of their furrows yet remains on the shoulders of very high hills, made when the ground was mostly wood and forest. I have seen how they gather into tribes and families; that they have children (though, I believe, only rarely), as well as nurses, midwives, musicians and many other things that show them to be not unlike us in any number of ways. I have heard it said that this is to mock us, but in my heart I do not believe that to be so.

• • •

As to other forms of housing, these are large and fair and (unless at some odd occasions) unperceivable by mortal eyes, like certain enchanted islands, having for light continual lamps, and fires, often appearing without fuel to sustain them. I may say that I have visited palaces of the utmost splendour, though they seemed still to be created from the most natural of elements, rather than the harsh brick and mortar of our world. Sometimes, I have wondered if the Faery races truly need any such habitation to live, since I have never observed them to sleep, or to engage upon the domestic duties that concern us so much. To be sure, they cook and weave and make music and live lives that seem to me to reflect those of the Lands

Above, yet there is a constant mystery about them, an inner life which remains as hidden to me as on that first day when I entered the Lands Beneath. One might ask: where do they go when they are not at play, or creating the many wondrous objects that I have glimpsed? To this question, I feel, I shall never know the answer, and perhaps it is anyway best left to their own knowledge.

The Seelie and Unseelie Courts

I find that the greatest race, the Sidhe, whom I have already encountered, is divided into two distinct courts. These go by the name Seelie (Blessed) and Unseelie (Unblessed), even among themselves. The Seelie court is the place from which those of Faery who are well disposed to humankind go out into our own world, for which in some places they are known as Trooping Faeries. Those who have no love for us, and it must be said that there are many of these, are the Unseelie, who continually seek to punish or harm us in any way they can. Long have I sought the reason for this, for they are reluctant to speak of it, and it was some time before I was to encounter them. However, I learned that there was a great divide in the races some long while since, in which those who sought to live in harmony with humankind elected to remain in one place while those who sought to make endless war upon us chose to go elsewhere. The Seelie courts are those to which I have been privy; the Unseelie I have but once ventured into, with what results shall be told in due time.

• • •

At the beginning of each quarter of the year the courts uproot themselves and remove to new lodgings, being restless by nature and reluctant to remain in one place, and finding some ease by the regular changing of habitation. At such times Seers, or those gifted with the second sight, may encounter them, even on the highways, and sometimes claim to find arrowheads, which they call elf-shot, fallen from the bodies or prey dispatched by the Faery folk as they pass by.

• • •

Those who are able to see the Faery races in this way generally refrain from travel abroad at those times of the year, and have made it a custom to go to church every first Sunday of the quarter to guard themselves, their corn and cattle, against any unchancy shadow of these wandering tribes of elfkind. However, I have noticed that often these same people will not been seen in church again till the next quarter, as if their piety were nothing more than protection against those arrows that fly in the dark.

The History of Faery

One day, not long after my first visit, I returned to the howe and requested of Kee that he should tell me something concerning the history of the races that lived below the earth. At first he was reluctant to answer, but then seemed to recall that he had been instructed to give me whatever help I might need in my efforts to learn more of the peoples of the Lands Beneath. Therefore, as we sat by the great well that lies close to the centre of the great cavern, I asked him concerning these things, and had, by way of response, a lengthy answer, which I have endeavoured to set down here as well as my poor memory will permit.

• • •

'We are an ancient people,' Kee told me. 'We were here long before your kind walked on this earth. We remember everything and have seen everything that took place here for many thousands of your years. We ourselves do not measure time as you do, so that for us time passes slowly. We do not speak of our origins to anyone not of our race, but it is certain that we emerged from the earth as you yourselves did, though much sooner in the history of the world.

'For a long time we were alone, save for the creatures who shared the world with us. In that time we lived above the earth, under the sun and moon and stars, which we loved to look upon. We dreamed and sang and told stories of the first days. We seldom mated and even less often gave birth, for we were and are a long-lived people, and our numbers remained constant for many hundreds of your years.

'Then one day we became aware of
those we called Newcomers, a strange
race who lived mostly in caves or holes
scraped from the earth. They were large
and slow of movement and wit, and,
as we swiftly learned, could be both
savage and cruel. They hunted the
great creatures with whom we
shared the land, and on one occasion
they hunted us – bringing the first
death to our people in many ages.'

Curse of the Newcomers

Only slowly, as I listened to these words, did it dawn upon me that the beings described by Kee were almost certainly our own ancestors, those poor savages that dwelled in caves and dressed themselves in the skins of animals. I could not help but feel sorrow in my heart to think upon those dark days. Thus I learned from my companion how at first they had been mindful to drive these brute folk out, even to kill them. But others spoke of moving from the places where these Newcomers dwelled into places where they would not come and of erecting barriers they might not cross. This policy won, and so the Faery races began a pattern of hiding that became second nature to them.

• • •

'To begin with,' Kee told me, 'we lived simply in the wild places, far from the territory of the Newcomers. But gradually, as they hunted further and further, we were forced to withdraw ever deeper into the land. At last we chose to go below the earth, making caverns for ourselves, lit by strange suns and moons, as you have seen. We became to you the People of the Hollow Hills, the Dwellers beneath the Mounds, the Faery People, the Little Dark Ones. But always we were the Sidhe.'

Those Who Walk Among Us

On this occasion I asked no more of my guide, though in the days that followed I have learned how the Faery folk have chosen to live both beside and among us. Thus when they choose, or when one of our kind is gifted with the Sight, they can be seen indeed, and sometimes they enter into our own lives in ways both subtle and mysterious.

• • •

Some that I have seen can take the form of a man or a woman, so that it appears as though the same person were in two places at the same time. The Faery themselves avow that everything in what they call the Great World, or the Lands Above, has another that resembles it. So that, just as there are fishes caught at sea that resemble monks in their hoods and robes, so there are strange and wondrous beings in their world that can resemble exactly those of our own, but are not. Human tales of good or bad daemons and guardian angels are said by them to be a mistake, sprung from this doubling or copying of man or woman.

These beings that choose to counterfeit us are called Coimimeadh or Co-walkers. They appear in every way like those beings they copy, whether man or woman, bird or beast, haunting them like shadows, sometimes seen and known both before and after the true person is dead. They may be seen to enter a house in such a way that the people who dwelled there, and knew the person of that likeness, could not tell them apart, save that they spoke not at all, but rather sat still by the fire, staring into the flames.

These copies return at last to their own place. They may accompany the living man or woman frequently, for ends best known to themselves, whether to guard him from the secret assaults of some of their own folk or as a sportful ape to counterfeit all his actions I do not know.

• • •

Certain stories seem to prove that faeries that possess light or airy bodies take pleasure in capering like sheep, or whistling and shrieking like unlucky birds, in every way aping the original forms they have copied. If invited, these companions will sometimes make themselves known to humankind and may even offer them assistance; otherwise, being in a different state and element to ourselves, they will not willingly converse with us.

Great-Eaters and Others

I have been much concerned with the manner of eating among the Faery people, for they seem to eat but little, yet still are strong and hale in their bodies. I have learned, though, that there is a tribe known as the Heluo or Great-Eaters. These are voracious elves known also as Joint-Eaters or Just-Halvers. They feed only on the essence of what men eat, because of which they are lean as herons, notwithstanding their devouring appetite. Yet it would seem they convey that substance elsewhere, for these Subterraneans eat but little in their dwellings, their food being clean, and served up by pleasant children like enchanted puppets.

What food they extract from us is conveyed to their homes by secret paths, as some skilful women can take the pith of milk from their neighbours' cows, into their own cheesehold. The cheese made of the remaining milk of a cow thus strained will swim in water like a cork. The method they use to recover their milk is by way of a bitter chiding of the suspected enchanter, charging them by a counter-charm to give back what they have stolen.

• • •

I have heard it said, most often among the people of Aberfoyle, that one should never eat the food of Faery. The reason given for this is generally that he who partakes of the food of the Subterranean races must stay for ever within the Faery kingdom. How this may be I have often wondered, and on the occasion of a recent visit to the Lands Beneath I took the opportunity to ask about the nature of the food eaten there.

My companion's answer, I must confess, surprised me. 'Our food is simple,' he said, 'and not unlike your own. We love barley meal best of all, and also stalks of heather, the milk of the red deer and goats. One of our greatest delicacies we call brisgen, which is the root of the plant you call silverweed.' He then went on to explain that the stealing of food is one of the greatest games they have. They do not steal because they need to, but for the joy of it. They call this action foison, and there is great delight to be had from it. Seeing perhaps a touch of disapproval in my look, Kee added, 'Of course we give back all that we take – sometimes more.'

'So,' said I, 'if I were to partake of the food of this land, might I still be able to leave?'

Kee smiled at me and beckoned me to follow him. We were standing, as I recall, on the side of a gently sloping hill. I followed Kee upward and at the top several large trees stood in a circle.

Beneath their shade was a table laid with a silken cover and adorned with the most beautiful silver plates and goblets of crystal. Each plate was piled high with delicacies, many of which I recognized, while others were unfamiliar. The goblets were filled to the rim with what seemed like pure water.

'Here is our feast,' said Kee. 'Will you eat?'

Faery Food

I must confess that I felt no small fear at this moment. If I refused I would surely insult my host, yet if I ate, and the stories were true, then I would be lost for ever to the world above and to my dear family. However, as I reflected, on no single occasion in my visits to the Lands Beneath had I ever felt threatened by my hosts. Surely if they intended to entrap me, they would long since have done so? And why, indeed, should they wish to do so? Surely there was nothing one man had to offer – least of all my humble self – that might in any way improve their lot?

◆ ◆ ◆

So it was that I advanced and took up what seemed the most recognizable thing: bread. I tore off a crust and found it still warm, as though but lately removed from an oven – but where was the oven? Thinking no more, I placed the scrap of bread in my mouth and tasted what must be the finest loaf ever created! Such was the wonderful quality of it that even now, seated in my study in the rectory, I can still taste it. I followed it with a sip of water – and found it to be as bright and clear as any I had ever known. Not even the clean, peaty water from the well in my garden tastes so fresh. At once I knew, and declared it to my companion, the truth of the stories told of Faery food. It was not that the food possessed any magical qualities to bind those who walked there, but the sheer delight of the tastes must make all who tried it long to return again for more.

Kee's eyes were bright. 'Some may find themselves tasting only dust and ashes,' he said seriously. 'But those of good heart may taste our food as it truly is.'

Thus I may say that I have tasted the food of Faery and lived to tell of it – for assuredly I am home now and not shut for ever in the Subterranean realm.

Faery Dress and Faery Speech

I have noted earlier that the apparel and speech of the Subterranean races are like those of the people and country under which they live: so they wear plaids and variegated garments in the Highlands of Scotland or the plaid cloths in Ireland. Their speech remains remarkable to human ears –

though it is heard but little since, to we mortals, they seem to speak in our own tongue. Yet as to their native dress, if so it may be termed, they spin very fine cloth, dyed with most varied shades, and they embroider; but whether it be from manual operation of substantial refined stuffs with apt and solid instruments, or only curious cobwebs, impalpable rainbows and aphantitic imitation of the actions of more terrestrial mortals, I leave to conjecture.

The Faery Nurse

Women are yet alive who tell that they were taken when in childbed to nurse Faery children, a hungry copy of their own infant being left in its place, like a reflection in a mirror, which, as if it were some insatiable spirit in assumed body, made first semblance to devour meat that it cunningly carried by, and left the carcass as if it expired, and departed the place as if by a natural and common death. The child is provided with milk and food, and all other necessaries are set by the nurse, but she neither perceives any passage out nor sees what these people do in other rooms of the lodging.

• • •

When the child is weaned, the nurse vanishes or dies, or is conjured back, or is given the choice of staying there. If any Subterranean be so subtle as to practise sleights for procuring

a privacy to their mysteries (such as making use of their ointments, which render them invisible, or cast them in a trance, or alter their shape, or make things appear at vast distance), they smite them with a puff of wind, and bereave them of both natural and acquired sights in the twinkling of an eye (both these being in the same organ and inseparable), and strike them dumb.

The local people put out bread or place iron in a woman's bed when travelling to save her being stolen. They commonly report the Faery beings are terrified by nothing earthly so much as by cold iron, though they can give no reason for it. (This I must remember to enquire of my hosts.)

• • •

An old woman, living in Aberfoyle, told me one such story of the appearance of a faery in human form, and what befell because of it. I shall relate it here, as I remember it, to illustrate the nature of the (sometimes treacherous) interaction between the Subterranean races and ourselves.

There was once a farmer and his wife living up the way from here. They had three children, and my story happened while the youngest was on the breast. The wife was a good wife enough, but her mind was all on her family and her farm, and she hardly ever went to the kirk without falling asleep, and she thought the time spent in the chapel was twice as long as it should be.

Late one night the farmer was wakened up by the cries of his children. He sat up and rubbed his eyes, but there was no wife at his side, and when he asked the little ones what was become of their mother, they said they had seen the room full of small men and women, dressed in white, and red, and green, and their mother in the middle of them, going out by the door as if she was walking in her sleep. Out ran the farmer and searched everywhere round the house, but neither tale nor tidings did he get of her for many a day thereafter.

About six weeks later, just as he was going out to his work, a neighbour who used to mind women at their lying-in came up to him, and kept step by step with him to the field, and this is what she told him.

'Just as I was falling asleep last night, I heard a horse coming up the lane and a knock at the door, and there, when I came out, was a fine-looking dark man, mounted on a black horse, and he told me to get ready in all haste, for a lady was in great want of me. As soon as I put on my cloak and things, he took me by the hand, and I was sitting behind him before I felt myself move. "Where are we going, sir?" says I. "You'll soon know," says he, and then he drew his fingers across my eyes and not a bit of sight remained in them. You may be certain I was afraid then, and that I knew he was one of the Faery kind. I kept a tight grip of him, and I never knew where we were going, nor how long we were about it, till my hand was taken again and I felt the ground under me.

'Then I felt his fingers go across my eyes again, and there we were before a castle door, and in we went through a big hall and great rooms all painted in fine colours, with green, red and gold bands, and ornaments, and the finest carpets and chairs and tables and window-curtains, and fine ladies and gentlemen walking about. At last we came to a bedroom, with a beautiful lady in bed, and there he left me with her; and it was not long till a fine bouncing boy came into the world. The lady clapped her hands, and in came the dark man, and kissed her and his son, and praised me, and gave me a bottle of green ointment to rub the child all over.

'Well, I rubbed the child sure enough, as I'd been told, but my right eye began to smart and I put up my finger and gave it a rub, and then I had a great fright, for suddenly I saw that the beautiful room was a cave, with water dripping down the walls, and the lady, the lord and the child seemed to be nothing but skin and bone, so thin were they, and the rich dresses looked like so many rags. I didn't let on that I found any difference, and after a bit the dark man says, "Go before me to the hall door, and I will be with you in a few moments, and see you safe home."

'Well, just as I entered the outside cave, who should I see watching near the door but your poor wife, Molly. She looked round all frightened and says to me in a whisper, "I'm brought here to give suck to the child of the King and Queen of the Faeries, but there is one chance of saving me. All the court will pass the cross by the road to Aberfoyle next Friday night, on a visit to the faeries of Eildon. If John can catch me by hand or cloak when I ride by, and has courage not to let go his grip, I'll be safe. Here's the

King now. Don't open your mouth to answer. I saw what happened with the ointment."

'The dark man didn't once cast his eye towards Molly and he seemed to have no suspicion of me. When we came out I looked about me, and where do you think we were but next to the Rath of Glen-na-Foyle. I was on the horse again, which looked not nearly as fine as it had before. Soon I found myself at my own door. The King slipped five guineas into my hand as soon as I was on the ground, and he thanked me and bade me good night. I hope I'll never see his face again.

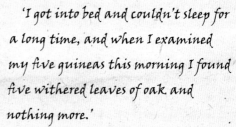

'I got into bed and couldn't sleep for a long time, and when I examined my five guineas this morning I found five withered leaves of oak and nothing more.'

Well, you may imagine the fright, the joy and the grief the poor man was feeling when the woman finished her story. They talked and they talked, and made a plan; and when Friday night came, both were standing where the mountain road crosses the one going to the Eildon Hills. The night was dark, but at last the midwife gave a start and said, 'Here they come, bridles jingling and feathers tossing.'

The farmer looked but could see nothing, while the woman stood trembling, with her eyes wide, looking down the road.

'I see your wife,' said she, 'riding on the outside just so as to be near us. We'll walk on quietly as if we suspected nothing and when they come past us I'll give you a push so that you're against them. Then it's up to you.'

Well, they walked on easy, their poor hearts beating in their breasts, and though he could see nothing, the farmer heard a faint jingle, and a tramping, and a rustling, and at last he got the push that she promised. He spread out his arms, and there was his wife's waist within them, and he could see her plain.

Then such a noise arose as if there was an earthquake, and he found himself surrounded by fearsome creatures, shouting at him and striving to pull his wife away. But he held his wife as if it was iron his arms were made of. Then, in the next moment, everything was as silent as the grave and the poor woman was lying in a faint in his arms.

Well, Molly made a good recovery and all in good time was minding her family again. But as for the midwife who helped her out, one day she was at the market, when what did she see walking among the tubs of butter but the dark man, very hungry-looking, taking a quiet scoop out of one tub or another.

'Oh, sir,' says she, 'I hope your lady is well, and the young child.'

'Pretty well, thank you,' says he, staring at her closely. 'How do I look in this new suit?' says he, standing to one side of her.

'I can't see you plain at all, sir,' says she.

'How now?' says he, getting round to the other side.

'Indeed, sir, your coat looks no better than a withered dock leaf.'

'Maybe it will be different now,' he said, and struck the eye she had rubbed with faery ointment with a switch.

After that she saw nothing more of the Faery people and ever after went quietly about her business and never told another soul what had happened, except for me.

◆ ◆ ◆

Such tales as this may well reflect the true nature of certain of the Faery race, but in my own wanderings in their country I have seen, with one exception, mostly kindness and gentleness, and a nobility which far outstrips our own. Yet, as I know also – to my cost – they will guard their secret world with the utmost determination, so that those who have not been invited as I was may well be punished, like the goodwife in the story.

Exiles from Eden

The more I am with them the more I have begun to detect in the Faery people a certain lingering sadness or sorrow, which, while it is a secret thing, is discernible when one has spent enough time in their company. On the surface they seem filled with laughter and the delight of dancing and song. Yet, when one observes them carefully, they are prone at times to fall silent and to grow still, and at such times I have glimpsed great sorrow in them. Even Kee, who seems at all times to radiate joyfulness, has displayed signs of this. I have not yet had opportunity, and indeed may never be so able, to ask the reason for this – to do so, it seems to me, would be to overstep the boundaries of politeness that are drawn between us. These boundaries, though invisible and without substance, are yet as real as if made of wood or stone. To cross them would, I have no doubt, bring instant censure upon me, perhaps even ensure that I was banned from returning to the Lands Beneath.

Thus I am left to ponder on this state of sadness among the dwellers in the Faery realms. Only one clue have I so far been given, in a conversation with Kee in which I asked for more details of the history of the Subterranean races.

'Much there is that we have forgotten,' said he, 'for we are an ancient people and, though our memories stretch back over many ages, we do not recall our origins. Once we had a home elsewhere, but whatever place it was is no longer known to us.'

It was in these words that I heard – or thought I heard – a lingering note of sorrow in the voice of my Faery companion. I believe I glimpsed at that moment a well of endless night that fell far beyond my own awareness.

◆ ◆ ◆

Is this, then, the reason for the sorrow I sometimes detect within myself when I am in the Lands Beneath? Are the Faery people exiled from their true home? And in what place might they once have dwelled? I recall a fragment of lore, told to me by one of the aged men of the parish. He had heard tell that the Faery race was once of a status not far from angels (as indeed I have myself felt at times) but that a day came when, for whatever reason, they were cast out from the heavenly realm, where they were at that time welcome. Since when they have lived a wandering, houseless existence and dwell in a constant state of exile.

◆ ◆ ◆

If this is true then it is small wonder if there be sympathy between our two races – for are we not also exiles from Eden? As our First Mother and First Father were cast out from the Garden of All Earthly Delights, so too, perhaps, were the Subterranean races. Of these things I may only speculate, yet I grow more certain each day of the shadow I have detected within them.

Bright Things

For a long while I believed that the Faery races did not have the skill of writing and that they therefore possessed no written history or literature. But on a recent visit to the Lands Beneath, upon seeing how Kee watched as I scribbled in this notebook, I was moved to ask if he understood what it was that I did.

'Indeed so,' was his reply. 'We use a similar means to record our most important things, though much we commit to memory since in that way it remains alive.'

'But surely writing would form a more permanent record?' I responded.

'We believe that to record something in this way is to kill its essence, so we seldom make use of this form, as you do so constantly.'

'But do you not have scholars or teachers who examine records of past things?' I asked, warming to my subject.

'We have lore-masters,' answered Kee. 'Those whose task is to remember the Bright Things.'

'What are these Bright Things?' I enquired, for this was not an expression I had heard before.

'The Bright Things are those things which are bright to us,' explained my companion patiently. 'Things that shine forth in our spirits and illumine our days. Surely you have such things in your world?'

I reflected upon this for a time, then ventured, 'We have tenets of belief, of faith – things we hold to be beyond question.'

'I am uncertain whether these are the same as our Bright Things, yet it seems to me that any things that bring joy whenever they are considered are bright, and contribute to all life. Such things do not need to be of substance or have form. If they are bright they are Known for Themselves, and are unbendingly true to the Wisdom of All Things. Is this not the same as you describe?'

Books of Light

While I thought more deeply on these matters Kee, in the way that all the Faery people seem able to do, brought me to a place I had not been before, though I was scarcely aware of having travelled at all. Indeed, let me record now that in all my journeys through the Lands Beneath I have almost never had any sense of travelling from place to place as when I am above ground. I might almost say that I had but to wish myself somewhere and there at once, or almost at once, I was. This is, it seems to me, part of the nature of the Subterranean realm, its subtlety being such that its very substance is constantly in a state of flux.

• • •

On this occasion, my companion brought me to a structure that resembled a fine building made of stone; though how exactly it was constructed I could not see, detecting no sign of masons' tools upon the stones or any kind of mortar. Yet the building stood, however improbably, in the midst of a place that seemed, somehow, richer than other places I have seen. By this I mean that where it stood the grass around it seemed a more intense green, and that the very air seemed to radiate a fine golden quality. Even the building itself seemed to emit a soft kind of glow. I know of no other words to describe this, other than to say that it 'shone'. Perhaps this is part of the 'brightness' to which Kee referred.

Now it was that we entered the building, to find ourselves in a spacious hall in which were many racks and shelves. Upon these sat row upon row of volumes, many bound in cloth or leather and tooled most exquisitely. My excitement knew no bounds, for I had at once a vision of myself translating these volumes of lore, as I once transcribed the word of God for the Gaelic people, so that they might be studied by those wiser than myself.

I looked with some anxiety at my companion and asked whether I might examine the books – fearing, in my heart, that he would say no. But, 'Of course,' said he, and with trembling hands I took down a volume with a particularly fine binding and, with swiftly beating heart, opened it.

There before me were words inscribed in the strong regularity of a scholar's hand – but all were written in a language unknown to me, in letters that seemed like no other I had ever seen. Not only that, but as I looked upon them it seemed that they danced before my eyes, almost as if made of light, shifting in some strange manner, so that where before they had formed one pattern, now they formed another.

In that moment, all hopes that I had entertained of returning to my own world with writings penned by the Faery races themselves were dashed. For even were I able to copy the letters, how could I be certain of their meaning, since what was written seemed to change constantly?

As though aware of my disappointment, Kee volunteered, 'I have noticed that the marks you make in your book remain unchanging. For us, every thought is so subtle it cannot be caught in this way. Thus we write but little, since there are so many

variations to every letter, every word, that they can
never be the same for more than a moment.
Once again, you express your desire to fix
things in one place. For us this is impossible –
everything in our world is constantly
changing. This is how we see things and how we
are able to sustain our long lives. Only you,
in the Lands Above, seek to fix all that you
see or feel, every thought or action, in one
place and for all time. We do not understand how you can do this,
or how you continue to live in such a way. It is one of the things
that make your kind and mine so very different.'

'Yet some things are written here, and placed in this building,'
I said.

'Indeed,' answered my companion, 'but these things are only
what your thoughts tell you, so that you may fix them. Our books
contain things that are eternal – yet even these change in form.
What you see here will be different again in but a brief moment of
time as you measure it.'

♦ ♦ ♦

Thus I found the writings of the Faery races and knew them lost to
me even as I gazed upon them. And though I have looked again for
the building that contained those books (if such they can truly be
called) I have never seen it again.

As with so much that I have been shown in the Lands Beneath,
it seems to have faded back into the very substance of the place as
though it had never existed.

Time and Place

Since I have visited the Lands Beneath I have learned to distrust the measurement of moment upon moment that we call time. I was told when I first entered the Faery howe that I could spend as much time in the Subterranean realm as I wished and yet return home with only the briefest of moments having passed, and this I have found to be true. Just how this is possible I cannot fathom, though I believe it may be something to do with the nature of the place, perhaps with its very substance. I realize for certain that in the Lands Beneath there really is no time – or at least not as it is understood by us mortals. Though I am aware of the passing of moment upon moment within myself, yet all around me there is both a stillness and a sense of fluidity that are not like this world of ours. I have even begun to suppose that everything I have seen became real because I observed it. It is even entirely possible that nothing I have described has any reality at all, at least not as we would understand it; rather that the Faery world exists in a state of constant potentiality, of becoming, so that objects, shapes, even worlds, appear because they are willed into being. I doubt that any man or woman now living will understand these things, but none the less I write them here – though they may seem to be the ravings of an aberrant mind – in the hope that one day they will be read by those who will perceive them as somehow important truths.

An Unwelcome Visitor

I have come to believe of late that the Faery folk may not be fleshly at all, but of some other substance entirely, unknown to man. To be sure the chief races, especially the Sidhe, have about them the appearance of human beings at times (at others, not!), being exceedingly fair of face and form and possessed of limbs and hair and features not unlike our own (though more refined). Yet I have observed that they are less substantial than us – as, indeed, is much of the Faery realm – and that, perhaps because of this, they are able to move through time and space in a manner not in the least like ourselves. I have heard it reported among the people of Aberfoyle that they are impossible to kill because of this. I imagine that few would attempt this, or wish it, but there will ever be those who seek to destroy what they fear or do not understand, and so I have heard of men who took up arms against the Subterranean races. One such, a farmer named H— who lived but a few miles from our church – described an encounter with one of those whom, from his imperfect description, I took to be one of the tribes, known as Sprigguns, who had

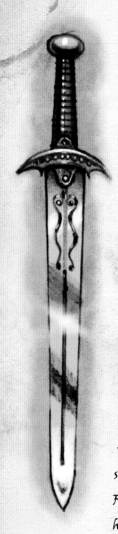

previously caused the man much grief (he claimed) by spreading murrain in his cattle and stealing from his hayricks and barns.

Finally, in desperation (or so he said) the man took down a rusty sword that had hung above his hearth from Flodden Field and lay in wait to catch the offending creature. 'I knew 'twas not of human flesh,' he said afterwards, 'for it flickered like a torch in the night, and when it had passed some food was missing or else some other trouble came to my beasts.' Well, it seems that around midnight on this day the farmer's patience was rewarded. He saw the flickering shape of his unwanted visitor crossing through his yard. At which the man jumped out and, with a mighty swipe of his old blade, he cut the creature in twain across the middle. Or so he later claimed, adding that the unearthly being vanished at once as if it had never been. As for the man himself, he reported an even stranger occurrence – that as he struck the creature he was himself transported several miles to a hillside, where he regained his senses. He found himself standing beneath an ancient gnarled tree, long believed to be a Faery marker, holding his sword, but with no memory at all of how he came to be there and, judging by the position of the moon, without any time having passed. Another curious detail he reported was that the blade of his sword, hitherto rusty, now shone bright as a star. Nor could he account for this, and though many people winked and tapped their heads knowingly and spoke of drunkenness, the man afterwards reported no further attacks upon his beasts or food store.

The Appearance of the Faery Realm

Now I have no means to judge what may be the truth of such matters, but there are things that I have observed while in the Lands Beneath that lead me to suppose that the Faery races are indeed composed of a different substance, because of which they are somehow enabled to transport themselves and others through touch. It may well be – or at least so I believe – that it is by this means that I myself have been permitted to journey through the Subterranean realm, though not by touching any of the Faery themselves (I have observed that they do not like to be touched at all by us) but rather by treading the very ground of the Lands Beneath.

• • •

More and more as I have journeyed in the Subterranean realm I have found that, while I might set forth or request to be taken in a particular direction, I have little or no memory of the journey. Thus I might wish to explore a region to the west, and find myself arrived there without any time (as I judge it) having passed, and with no sense of having walked upon a road, or traversed hill, valley or stream. Yet all of these features I have observed to exist in this strange land, so that I wonder often if it is not the working of my own mind that creates these things around me, landmarks as it were, that serve to make me feel more comfortable in a place that truly looks not at all like the world above.

Several times I have tried to shut out my normal everyday perceptions and to see how the Lands Beneath might really appear, but each time I have been unable to do so. Once, for the briefest of moments, I believed myself to be walking in a liquid place, formless as the very air, yet somehow shaped by the actions of the subtle minds of the Faery race. But of this I can say no more at this time, since it was but an immeasurable glimpse and may have been no more than my own imagination, shaping what I sought to understand. I must confess that this aspect of the Lands Beneath remains as great a mystery as ever, and I doubt that I shall ever know more of it than this.

Faery Wives and Lovers

On the matter of the corporeality or otherwise of the Faery races, I have lately had occasion to speak of this matter with my companion and guide, Kee. On reading over these rough notes, I came upon the remarks concerning the history of the people of the Lands Beneath that Kee himself had made to me not long after my first venture into the Faery howe. Here he had mentioned that while they were long-lived they seldom reproduced, so that their numbers remain stable. This brought to mind the story of the midwife which I recounted earlier and in addition the many tales I have heard of faeries and mortals marrying (though often all too briefly and with sorrowful outcome). Today I asked Kee about the relationship which exists between us. I mentioned that I had heard stories about contracts made between human and Sidhe, and how human men have loved Sidhe women and vice versa. I sought, as delicately as possible, to question Kee about such unions, and was rewarded with the following comments.

'It is true that our species have intermingled from time to time,' answered my companion, smiling a little as I thought. 'Both our species are subject to the same laws that result in a meeting of kind with kind. We too know the pangs of love and have been drawn to your species on occasions. We feel very strongly that one of the reasons for our existence here in this place is to learn about love, which we believe is a very misunderstood emotion.

'We have seen so much hatred in your world, much suffering caused by misguided affection or the denial of love. Yet we have been judged by you to be passionless, cold, reserved. This is far from the truth. Many of my people have shared love for ages without stinting. Among humankind it seems that love has been fragmented into so many different channels that it has become weakened. You spoke of a contract, and that indeed is one of the central aspects of love. It establishes a bond that is deeper than words, a bond that should endure and be honoured despite the tests that it must undergo.'

Kee paused for a moment, and I thought I detected a note of that general sadness that I feel is present within all the Faery races. Then he continued, 'When the universe as we each know it emerged, it was whole and complete, harmonious and sounding a resonant note. Each and every thing, every being and species, uttered a sound that harmonized with each other. They formed a song that was more beautiful than we can imagine. But gradually, notes of disharmony crept into the song. There were those within every species, our own included, who became unable to recognize the note they produced. This led to greater and greater unbalance and disharmony, and within the shape of the universe many things came into being then that added to this disharmony. After this everything changed. Even we, who once existed within that great harmony, have heard notes that strike deeply within us and cause great pain. Perhaps it could be said that one of the tasks of both our species is to find their true note and sound it once again.'

• • •

These comments, which I have attempted to record as best I can in my own poor words, continue to speak to my own heart, and bring to mind a story that I heard told among the people of Aberfoyle which, I believe, shows how hard such contracts may be for both races.

The Lady from the Lake

It seems there was a young man, the son of a poor widow, who was out one day, watching their few poor cows, which liked to graze by the side of a lake not far from here. As the boy walked there, he saw a most beautiful woman sitting on the surface of the

water, combing her long hair. At once the boy fell in love with her and offered her some of his plain barley bread. But the woman refused, telling him his bread was too hard. Next day he went back to the lakeside again and offered her a perfectly baked loaf. This time she smiled upon him, and with his heart in his mouth he asked her to be his bride. 'I will marry you,' said she, 'on one condition – that you never strike me. Three blows are all that it will take to send me away.'

Well, the boy promised, and so the beautiful woman from the lake came to live with him. With her she brought many sheep, cattle, oxen and horses, and with these the wealth of the young man grew rapidly. Soon they had three sons, and a good house with fine linen and good grazing for their growing herd of cattle. But one day, as the lady was about to go riding, she asked her husband to bring her gloves. He did so, but when he gave them to her, he slapped her playfully with them. 'That is the first blow,' she said, but nothing more.

Years passed and the man grew older. The sons given him by the lady left home and went their way in the world. The man's luck continued to increase, along with his fortune and the respect in which he was held. Then one day he and his wife – who never seemed to become any older – were invited to a wedding. During the celebration, the lady from the lake was seen to weep long and hard. Her husband, embarrassed, shook her by the shoulder. 'Why do you weep?' he demanded. 'More sorrow will come of this day than joy,' she said, and then added, 'That was the second blow.'

Now the man was very careful indeed not even to raise his voice to his wife, for he loved her just as much as ever, and feared that he might accidentally drive her away. Then the day came when the couple went to the funeral of an old friend. Everyone stood by the graveside sadly, many weeping openly, but the lady was seen to laugh so much that she could not remain still. Shocked by this, the man took her by the arm and pulled her away. In doing so he was rougher than he intended. The lady looked upon him sadly. 'Joy begins with the end of life,' she said. 'But no more joy for us – for that was the third blow and our contract is broken.'

Despite the man's pleas, the lady made her way back to the lake. Behind her went all the sheep, cattle, oxen and horses – and their offspring, born in the years the couple had been together. All vanished away into the lake, leaving the husband a sadder and wiser man.

Now, I have no doubt that this lady was of the Faery kind, and that the seeming harshness of her actions was but part of the law by which all of the Subterranean races govern their lives. For I have seen, during my sojourns there, that they are above all things fair and honourable in their dealings with each other, to a degree that we mortals might find hard to accept. Indeed, their ways in this are still strange to me, though I cannot help but admire their scrupulous nature. There is very clearly a code by which they live, and though its exact nature remains hidden from me, yet I have no doubt that they hold dear to it at every point. May I never have occasion to be subject to this law, for I doubt not that it would overthrow all matters of friendship or familiarity.

Faery Gold and
Faery Weapons

It has long been known that the Faery races were exquisite craftspeople, and to this I can now bear witness, having seen for myself the rare and delightful objects of which they are capable. I had of course noted about the persons of those of the Subterranean lands a bright armada of decoration: bracelets, armbands, cloak pins and the like, as well as those great neck-rings of the kind called torques in the Gaelic speech. All of these objects were made of the finest yellow gold, intricately chased and besprinkled with precious stones.

Among the Sidhe race especially, there is a great pride in weapons and personal adornments, and I have observed the most wonderfully crafted swords with jewelled hilts and intricately engraven blades. Yet, when I asked and was given permission to handle one of these, I found it to be extraordinarily light, as though by some skill unknown to human smiths the Faery craftspeople knew how to make the metals in which they worked to be of less substance.

• • •

Two matters I felt called upon to raise with my host: one was the widely held belief that all metals are inimical to the Faery race, hence the placing of iron about the person of a young mother to prevent her child from being stolen; and the other, that I had often heard tell of 'Faery gold' that turned to smoke or dust when exposed to the air of the Lands Above.

Kee, to whom I addressed these questions, laughed when he heard them. 'It is true that, as you have been told, we do not like cold iron. Our remembrancers (a term most closely allied to our idea of historian) say that when the first races of you humans arrived here they brought with them weapons of iron, against which we had no protection when above the earth. For this reason, we were afraid of the metal that burned us. But in time we mastered the skill of working in iron and, though our smiths still prefer bronze or gold, they can make a true blade of iron, as you have seen. We see gold and bronze as honourable metals for weapons. For with an iron blade you may strike and strike again without let, but with a blade of gold or bronze the combatants can break off and straighten their blades and rest.

'As to Faery gold, you must know by now that not everything you see here is as it seems. Some things there are of ours that may simply melt away when the air of the Lands Above touches them, or when their purpose is accomplished.'

I felt – not for the first time, nor indeed the last – that my companion was having fun at my expense when he said these things. As I have written elsewhere in this book, I believe that much of what I have seen here derives in part from my wish to see it. Perhaps this too is the origin of the stories that things brought out of Faery cannot last in this world.

Faery Smiths

While on the subject of the Faery smith craft and weaponry, I have noticed that though certain of the races, such as the Sidhe, have craftspeople capable of making many strange and wondrous things, when it comes to the crafting of weapons they employ others to be their smiths. The particular creatures that fulfil this capacity are known as Kobbold, a kind

of small brown creature of leathery skin and small red-rimmed eyes. These beings live in caves, in what I believe to be the south of the Lands Beneath. (Though, as I have remarked before, direction is almost as hard to determine as is time or distance.) On approaching these caves, one hears at first a faint tapping, which grows gradually louder until it is a veritable cacophony of sound – produced, as I now know, by the beating of scores of tiny hammers upon small anvils.

• • •

On my most recent visit to the Lands Beneath, Kee took me to see these redoubtable workers. He had warned me beforehand that, while they were in nowise hostile, the Kobbold were less friendly than his own people towards humankind. 'Be careful that you touch nothing of their tools or the artefacts they work upon,' he told me. 'To do so can bring only anger and pain upon you.'

In fact, when I came to enter one of their caves – which I found to be larger than expected, and filled with the clamour of iron – it seemed that the Kobbold were so intent upon their work that I might have been no more than an insect. The caves were less brightly lit than most places I had visited in the Lands Beneath, and by far the strongest light came from the dozens of hearths built upon the floor of the cave. By this flickering light I saw many of the Kobbold, none more than four feet tall, labouring over objects that varied from swords to the most intricate adornments such as any woman in the Lands Above would prize above all others. Many tapped away with diminutive hammers and even finer tools upon sheets of gold or silver, impressing upon them patterns and shapes almost too varied for my poor eyes to fathom. Others worked over swords and spearheads, shaping them deftly into forms that looked as though they might cut the wind itself, forging the metal again and again, quenching it to great hissing and gouts of steam. It crossed my mind then to wonder for what use, other than decoration, these subtle blades were intended. But when I spoke of this to Kee, he shook his head silently and looked, if such an expression could be imagined on such a guileless face, uncomfortable. Even now, as I write these words back in my library in Aberfoyle, I cannot help but wonder if there is not some dark secret of the Lands Beneath that is being kept from me. Can it be that the Sidhe have enemies other than mankind? Or that those whom they refer to as 'Unseelie' hold grievances not only against the human race but also against those who would welcome us into the Lands Beneath? These thoughts concern me more than I can say.

◆ ◆ ◆

The world into which I have looked is so fair a place that I cannot imagine it torn by strife. The very name by which the Faery races are often known in the Lands Above – the People of Peace – suggests that this is an important aspect of their nature, and in all my studies and reading, as well as in my conversations with my Faery hosts, I have never heard mention of warfare. Rather they deploy their weapons in feats of skill and in friendly contests. I must somehow find out the truth of this – though I am aware that I must be careful if I do not wish to turn the goodwill of my hosts against me.

The Kobbold

I have learned more about the Kobbold that I must record here. Although they are so skilled in the making of weapons and adornments, they themselves will have none of them. They are miners as well as craftspeople, loving nothing more than to bring forth the veins of ore that are found everywhere in the Lands Beneath. It seems that this was always their great skill and that only lately (as the Faery races judge it) have they been called upon to acquire the skill of smithying. Though my companion spoke only briefly of this, I have cause to wonder whether this may be further evidence of my belief that there is tension between the Seelie and Unseelie courts. I hope with all my being that this may not be so, for I could not bear to see this fair and wondrous place stained by such a human-seeming activity.

Further to this, I must make note that, beyond their rich works of gold and bronze and silver, the Kobbold used once to make weapons of stone: spearheads, axes and suchlike, all carved with incredible delicacy from hard stone or from the soft yellow flint that is mined here in the north. Farmers, who refer to them as 'elf-shot', have turned many of these arrowheads up from ploughed soil. Those of antiquarian learning greater than mine have claimed that our ancestors made these. But I know better, for the Kobbold made them all.

Elf-shot and the Sight

Now that I have learned so much about the Subterranean races, I am more inclined to believe the stories told to me by labouring men and women. Above all, that many possess the Sight with which to see the Faery people. One cause of this, I am informed by my companion from the Lands Beneath, is being wounded, either deliberately or accidentally, by a Faery weapon – most often, I believe, an arrowhead. Once a man has been so struck, he cannot help but see the one who shot him and others of the same kind. Thus, the Subterraneans are at pains not to wound any mortal, since they are then able to perceive the goings and comings of the Faery people.

It seems also that, while our weapons may indeed have no effect upon them, as in the story already related, they may strike us with their elf-shot without our knowing or feeling hurt. The chief effect is a sudden ability to see the Faery people, though it may also be the cause of strange or unseemly behaviour. When horses bolt unexpectedly, or people are unneighbourly or transgress boundaries, this may be the effect of elf-shot. For it is certain that these arrows go between the worlds, and when they strike they may cause all kinds of disturbance. I have even heard tell of a man who became famous throughout Scotland and the Isles for curing people suspected of being elf-shot. He would search the bodies of those so affected, looking for tiny holes. When he discovered these, he would insert his finger or press upon the spot, and seemingly through the simple warmth of the human spirit draw forth the hidden missile and bring the man or woman out of their affliction.

Now this is of great interest to me, since it shows once again, as I have observed before, that objects coming out of the Lands Beneath may have a peculiar effect upon the mortal world. It seems that these things do not mix and that whenever a mortal man or women comes in contact with something from the Lands Beneath they are changed by it.

This is not to say that all instances of the second sight or seership are brought about in the manner described above, but it may well account for those where humans have seen the Faery even when they did not wish to be seen. This of course is of special interest to myself, since I have been allowed to see so much by the will of the Subterranean races themselves.

Guardians of the Trees

Today I visited the realm of the Sylvan elves, a race of the Faery people who are connected most especially with the natural world. My visit began when I asked Kee about the flora of the Subterranean realm. From the start I had noticed that many plants bloomed in the Lands Beneath that were not common in my own world. They added to the sense that so frequently came upon me, that this was truly another world in which I journeyed;

that it was not simply a place beneath the earth, but somehow existed in another way entirely.

Whether this be true or not remains to be seen, but my interest in the flora of the Subterranean realm grows apace. I have asked, and been granted, permission to make drawings of the plants that are of no known species, but on this occasion, when I asked about a particular flower that seemed only to grow close to the Great Hall of the Faery King and Queen, Kee answered that it would be more fitting to speak with the Sylvan race, who care for all such things.

Therefore we set off and – in the way of the Faery realms – found ourselves quite soon entering a stretch of woodland that rapidly deepened into something like a forest. I noticed at once that it had a look of the ancient world about it, which set it apart from the woods and groves I have visited elsewhere.

Paths there were to be sure, but they seemed more winding than in any such place that I have been, as though they wove a net that was more of the trees' devising – a way to confuse any mortal foolish enough or brave enough to enter there.

• • •

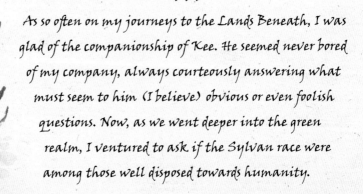

As so often on my journeys to the Lands Beneath, I was glad of the companionship of Kee. He seemed never bored of my company, always courteously answering what must seem to him (I believe) obvious or even foolish questions. Now, as we went deeper into the green realm, I ventured to ask if the Sylvan race were among those well disposed towards humanity.

'Indeed,' was his answer, 'save when you humans have
ventured too far into the forests and hurt the trees by
cutting or felling them with your sharp axes.'

'But surely,' I replied, 'this wood where we walk is
part of the Lands Beneath, where no axe of man may fall.'

Kee turned his great golden eyes upon me. 'This place is
not like others within the lands,' he said. 'Where we
walk is at once in both realms.'

'How may this be?' I asked, looking around me with
astonishment. For now that my companion had
informed me of the nature of the woodland, I began to
notice that the air in the great wood was different from the
still, quiet, almost breathless quality that characterizes the air of
the Subterranean realm.

'It is really quite simple,' replied Kee patiently. 'Here the veil
that disguises our world from yours is much thinner. It is the
nature of all green and growing things that they draw every
aspect of the created worlds closer to each other.'

As he spoke I experienced what I may only call a vision.
Looking ahead into the depths of the forest, I thought for a moment
that I saw the roots of another wood, one that grew in the Lands
Above, descending from the invisible dome of the sky in thin,
shimmering tendrils. Very ghostly they seemed, but though
insubstantial they were yet somehow vibrant with life. I believe,
thinking back upon this, that I may indeed have glimpsed my
own world as it must appear to the Faery races – a strange
insubstantial place, where all seems made of smoke or dreams.

An Elvish Garden

With this realization came a further flood of sensations. I found myself tasting the air, recognizing qualities within it that I had hitherto ignored. It was as though, with the blending of the two realms, I was more fully able to identify and to appreciate the subtle differences between them. And I understood that, within the Lands Beneath, the air was possessed of a wine-like quality, as though one might almost drink it down, and this is mirrored by a certain clear brightness of the air in parts of the Lands Above.

• • •

Where we walked now, I breathed in a heady bouquet of odours – the rich green of the loam and mast beneath our feet, mixed with a slightly resinous scent which seemed, not surprisingly, to issue from the trees around us.

Looking towards the arboreal splendour of the place, I saw an astonishing richness of flora – mighty oaks, beech, chestnut, birch and pine rubbed shoulders with ash, apple and willow, their deep-hued leaves all with a gloss upon them that seemed, as did so much within the Faery realm, brighter and somehow more alive than the very same things in my own world.

As I looked, I began to understand something of what my companion had said – for these were the trees of the lands above indeed, growing in far greater profusion and with many more species together in one place. A wonder such as I can only imagine may occur in one of the great royal gardens devised by the Tradescant brothers for His late Majesty.

When I made some comment to this effect, Kee smiled. 'It can be said that the Sylvan race are in some sense gardeners. All things that grow and have roots are in their care.'

As he spoke we arrived at an opening in the trees and I found myself standing at the entrance to what was, in every sense, a hall, though its walls were of living trees and its roof of branches that seemed almost woven naturally, as if the trees had willingly shaped themselves to that form.

But, while I was filled with wonder at the sheer scale of the place – I could not actually see how far it stretched, like a vast palace of silvery trunks and golden leaves – I had eyes only for the beings who moved slowly about the open space before us.

I knew at once that these were the Sylvan elves, and that they were at least related to the Sidhe folk, but there was about them a willowiness that reflected both the strength and the fragility of the world over which they watched.

Some were taller even than the tallest Sidhe I had seen so far, maybe as much as eight feet, and their hair – if hair it truly was – seemed more like twigs, as did their fingers, which were long and thin like the branches of hawthorn or ash. Others were shorter, statelier, and moved with greater slowness and purpose, while still others had quick, dainty movements that reminded me of the fluttering leaves of summer blossoms. There was, too, an extraordinary richness of colour about them, varying from deep green to blue, red, and even some that brought to mind the bark of birch trees. I realized also that I could not easily tell if these colours were clothing or skin.

Their faces, as I observed them, seemed strange to me, further from human than were even the Sidhe folk, who despite their beauty and grace had something of human shape about them. Some of the Sylvans possessed great eyes that resembled nothing so much as still pools of water, such as one might come across on the high moorland, or equally within the woodlands of the upper world. Such a variety of shapes, colours and forms was there, but even now, as I write these words, I am aware that I have forgotten more than I can remember.

Each one went about some task or other, and as I looked I saw indeed how they could well be seen as gardeners, for they were concerned with small living, growing things. I saw elves tending young shoots of almost every species I could remember, from tender ferns to hardy blaeberries.

• • •

Now I saw this mysterious place for what it was – a nursery where plants were tended with all the care and attention that would be lavished upon a human infant. What I had first taken for an unevenness of the ground, or for a strange patchwork quality, was in fact a vast carpet of living things, each in its own separate plot, every one of which was looked after by a Sylvan elf.

Kee led the way, weaving in and out of the intricate patchwork of garden plots to where a tall elf knelt on the earth, tending with the utmost grace a plant I recognized as that which

I had enquired after. I watched with great fascination as the
Sylvan wound its hands in and around the leaves and stem, petals
and stamens, of the plant – here pressing lightly, there apparently
stroking the plant. As it (I cannot say he or she, as the Sylvans

seem devoid of gender) did so, I saw what looked like sparks of light issuing from the ends of the twig-like digits and being absorbed into the plant. It was indeed as though the elf were somehow feeding the plant, which seemed to glow with each fresh infusion of energy.

Kee and I stood silently by until at length the Sylvan was satisfied with its work and stood up. I was forced to look upward into the face of this most glorious being, for it was, when standing, some eight to ten inches taller than I (who am of modest stature). I found myself gazing into the most extraordinary face, smooth about the brows and cheeks, yet elsewhere seamed with what I can only describe as bark-like wrinkles. The eyes were almost completely circular and were without pupil or iris, being wholly dark – though at the same time somehow glowing.

When the elf spoke, its voice possessed an almost flute-like quality, as though it might at any moment burst into song. This voice wove such a spell of harmony and quiet within me that I cannot now recall what words were spoken – or even indeed if any were. I can only remember the essence of what was relayed to me – that Kee had informed the elf (when and how, for I had heard no speech pass between them?) of my interest in this particular plant. The elf then spoke of it for some time, but in a way I cannot imagine even the most dedicated gardener in the Lands Above using. Rather, the elf described the qualities of the plant as a father might those of one of his children – for this, I quickly realized, was the relationship between them. The plant's nature was outlined as if it were indeed a sentient being. It had, I learned, a name, though I can neither pronounce nor write it here, and its especial quality was that at certain times of the day it emitted a perfume of great delicacy and sweetness, as though it could be said to be offering its scent to the very air of the Lands Beneath.

I listened in wonder as the Sylvan spoke on, describing the most subtle shades of scent as though they were colours upon an artist's palette. Would that I could even begin to recall all that was said, but most was beyond my clumsy mind to lay hold of in any way. As the elf spoke, I was aware of such a feeling of love issuing from this extraordinary being that I found myself bathed in it. If only those of my small flock in the Lands Above would bring even a tenth of such loving kindness to the House of God as this being, who in my world would have been called evil because it was unlike others, the world would be a better place.

The expression of this love was so overwhelming that I felt tears come to my eyes, and my thoughts turned to my own dear family. If some day, I thought, they might see what I have seen, hear what I have heard! And hard upon the heels of this thought came another. Would they indeed believe what I write here? Perhaps the time may come when I can show this writing to them, for I am certain they would be as deeply entranced by the Lands Beneath as am I. Yet I fear it may never happen, if I am to retain my place in the world of men.

Fern Seed and Invisibility

Of a certainty, there is no more well-known factor in all the tales told of Faery than that those who live there possess the ability to appear and disappear at will. I have long pondered upon this, having witnessed it several times in the Lands Beneath, but after my visit to the Sylvan elves a fragment of lore, told to me by some parishioner of mine, came to mind. This concerned the fact that on Midsummer's Eve, a time long held to be special to the Faery race, they gather the seeds of a particular type of fern, and that these, when held in the hand, do cause invisibility. It is even said, as I now recall, that mortal men and women may seem to fade from sight if they are able to catch such wondrous seeds, and therefore they go out on the eve of Midsummer to attempt this very thing. Some, I believe, are said to have succeeded in this, but I know of no one who has done so. Be that as it may, I took occasion to ask my companion of this mysterious fern. His answer was, as so often, delivered with a laugh.

'These are but playthings for our young,' he replied. 'We ourselves have no need of them, but since the ability to do what you describe does not occur in our race until we are older, we permit the use of such toys.' He paused a while, then continued, 'See, I have some of the very seed about me now.'

From somewhere within his garments Kee pulled forth a small bag tied about the neck with golden twine. Opening this, he scattered a number of tiny seeds into his shapely palm. To me they looked like any other seeds, save that perhaps they had about

them a certain glow –
but so much of the
Subterranean realm
possesses this glow
that I scarce took
notice of it. I looked
at my companion
expectantly, as
though he might
vanish in that
moment.

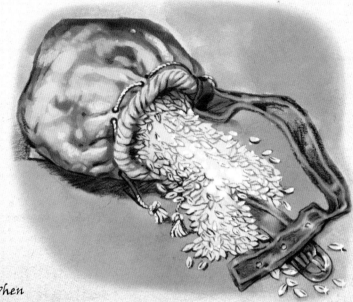

   'They only work when
they are placed on the back of the
hand,' he said, and held out the dusting of seeds towards me.

   For a moment only I hesitated, then there came to me such a
childish sense of delight in the possibility that I might experience
for myself what it felt to be invisible that I held out my hand,
palm downward, and allowed Kee to scatter a few of the seeds upon
it. At once I felt a strange prickling in the skin of my hand, which
spread rapidly to my arm and shortly throughout my whole body.

   Then gradually an even stranger sensation occurred. For as I
looked down at my hand and arm, I saw them fade – not
completely, but so that I was able to see the ground through them!
Bending my head so that I could see more of my body, I saw the
same thing occur. Only for a moment did this continue before I was
returned to normal – yet in that moment I knew myself to be all
but invisible!

Seeing the wonder in my face, Kee smiled.
'Such things are not for mortals,' he said.
'Sadly your kind would use such abilities to
do harm, to steal – even to kill.'

• • •

I forbore to mention the many stories told of the
Faery races using this very gift to steal, if
nothing more, for I remembered how Kee had told me
that whenever the Faery stole from us, they were determined to
give back more than they took. Perhaps such things are indeed no
more than games to them, as I have thought before. Yet I shall not
forget the wonder of this moment, and as I write these words I find
it hard to believe that I was myself quite vanished away but a
short time since.

The Phenoderee

Today I met the only being to be exiled from the Lands
Beneath and to be allowed to return! He is the Phenoderee,
a most remarkable creature towards whom I feel a great warmth
and liking. I had been discussing with Kee the question of those
who were permitted to enter the Subterranean realm, and not
unnaturally thought to ask about my own presence there. Kee
answered that the decision was mostly that of the King and
Queen, though the matter had been long debated in council.

'As you were told, we have long been aware of your interest in our affairs, and since there are those in our world who would seek to be better known and more truly represented, it was decided that you should be admitted.'

I then asked if he had heard of others like me who had been admitted to the Lands Beneath.

'Many have simply stumbled into our world,' answered Kee. 'However, most of these have been banished immediately, for we do not like to be observed, and many of your kind seek only to steal our gold or discover the secrets of our magic.'

This last was said without malice and I took no umbrage from it. But it was this that prompted me to ask whether any of the Faery race had ever been sent away from the Lands Beneath.

Kee hesitated for a moment before replying. 'There is one who transgressed our laws and was exiled to your world for many years. In time he returned, but he chooses to dwell alone, far from the court.'

At once my interest was piqued. I begged Kee to tell me more, though I could see that the matter made him ill at ease.

'He is the Phenoderee,' my companion answered. 'He fell in love with a mortal woman, many hundreds of your years ago, and was banished because of it. He lived out his life on earth for many years and afterwards returned.'

Again I felt some hidden sorrow in Kee's voice – no more than a hint, to be sure, but there none the less.

'But surely,' I said, 'we have spoken before of marriages between your kind and mine. How was this different?'

'It was not because he chose someone from your race,' said Kee.
'He refused to return when the King and Queen commanded it.
Instead he chose to live in the Lands Above, and for that reason he
was banished.'

Greatly daring now, I asked if I might see this being who
had lived in my world for so long.

Kee nodded his consent. 'But I must warn you,' he said, 'the Phenoderee may not wish to speak with you.'

On this understanding, we set out, and once again I marvelled that we could travel what seemed a great distance across the Lands Beneath without tiring and without more than the briefest amount of time having passed.

The Exile

Our way led us to higher ground than I had visited before in the Lands Beneath. After crossing a harsh landscape of stone and shale, and scrambling up the steep hillside, we found ourselves standing before the entrance to a large cave, from the mouth of which a plume of smoke drifted lazily into the still air. With it came the most mouth-watering cooking smell, something I had never detected before in the Lands Beneath.

As we drew near, a figure appeared at the entrance to the cave, shading his eyes against the light. He was short and stocky, though by no means as small as the Kobbold. His hair was long and very black, falling in tangles over his broad shoulders. He looked immensely strong and his expression was grim. Dark eyes regarded me with suspicion.

Kee stepped forward and, to my surprise, spoke in my own tongue. I was used to the Faery races addressing each other in their own speech, so this was unusual.

'I bring you a visitor from the Lands Above,' said Kee.

'So I see,' answered the Phenoderee. His voice was deep and measured, and his eyes never left my face.

'This is Robert Kirk,' said Kee. 'He walks among us at the command of the Lord and Lady.'

Not knowing in what way I should greet this being, on impulse I held out my hand. The Phenoderee regarded it with curiosity, then, to my surprise, reached out and clasped it briefly in his own strong, brown hand.

'Be welcome to my house,' he said, though I saw no lessening of the distrust in his eyes.

Kee bowed low and declared that he would leave us alone for a time, but that he would return for me later.

The Phenoderee nodded curtly and then stood aside from the cave mouth, beckoning me inside. I entered, not really knowing what to expect, and found myself in a room that, though sparsely furnished, was oddly reminiscent of a poor house in my own world.

A table and chair stood to one side, a low frame bed on the other. Skins were spread across the floor, and an elaborate lamp, which gave forth a warm glow like that which lit the Subterranean realm, hung from the ceiling. Close to the door was a small hearth, over which was suspended a cauldron. It was from there that the wonderful aroma came, and I felt my mouth water again as I smelled it.

'I live simply,' said the Phenoderee. 'But you are welcome to share my food.'

'My thanks to you, good sir,' I answered, uncertain, I must admit, how to proceed with this curious being.

Dinner in the Lands Beneath

*H*e ushered me to the solitary chair, then produced a second one from the back of the cave. I sat and watched as he moved about the cave, finding two rough bowls, some spoons and cups which he filled with water from a jug. All of these things had about them a plainness I had not seen anywhere else in the Lands Beneath. Were it not for the strange, unearthly light that flooded in from outside, and the fact that we were sitting in a cave, I might have believed myself to be back in my own world.

The Phenoderee set two bowls filled with a most delicious stew on the table and invited me to eat. I will long remember the taste of the food, which seemed, like so much else in the Lands Beneath, to be enhanced beyond anything I had tasted in the Lands Above.

We ate in silence, but several times I felt my strange host studying me. When at length we were done, the Phenoderee took out a long clay pipe, filled the bowl with aromatic tobacco and lit it. He offered some to me and, when I declined, leaned back in his chair and said, 'It is a long time since I spoke with anyone from your world. I have forgotten what it was like to do so.'

'May I ask how long ago it was that you were in the Lands Above?' I asked.

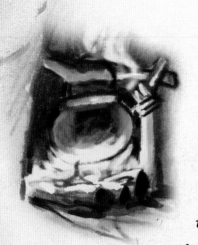

'In terms of your years, more than three hundred,' answered the Phenoderee. He sighed and stretched his limbs, and looked directly at me for the first time since I entered the cave. He said, 'Speak to me of your world. I should like to hear what changes have taken place there since I was last there.'

So we sat together, companionably, while I told the Phenoderee all that I could about my world as it was now. Occasionally my host would interrupt with some question – mostly concerning the tilling of the soil, which he seemed glad to discover had changed but little since he walked the earth.

After a time we fell silent, and I found the courage to ask my host if he would tell me of his own time in my world.

'Ah, that was long ago,' he said at last. 'Then I was known as a spirit of the harvest among the people of your world. They liked to employ me, for it was known that I could lay flat a field of standing wheat, flail it and stack it in a night. I could herd sheep and cattle too, and I cleared stones from the fields and carried them miles away in a night. They used to call me a force of nature, a little giant. They even made a song about me.'

To my surprise, he began to sing in a somewhat rusty but not unpleasant baritone. I write what I can remember of the song here, and will look for it again among the records of the Lands Above when I have the time.

'Phenoderee went at dawn to the round-field,
And skimmed the dew like cream from a bowl;
The maiden's herb and herb of the cattle,
He was treading them under his naked sole.

He was swinging wide on the floor of the meadow,
Letting the thick swath leftward fall;
We thought his mowing wonderful last year,
But the strength of him this year passes all!

He was lopping the blooms of the level meadow,
He was laying the long grass ready to rake;
The bog-bean out on the rushy curragh,
As he stroked and mowed it was fair ashake!

The scythe that was at him went whizzing through
  all things,
Shaving the round-field bare to the sod,
And whenever he spotted a blade left standing
He stamped down with his heel and unshod!'

Healing Given

The Phenoderee ended his song and looked at me in silence for a moment. Then he took a great breath and said, 'I was not too shy to start work at daybreak and let myself be seen and admired in the grey light of dawn. I attacked my jobs like a convulsion of nature, making the hard ground soft and the soft ground softer.

When I mowed I flung the grass to the morning star or the paling moon without heed of the cock's kindly word of warning from the nearby farmyard. I could clear a dinner in an hour and want nothing better than a crock full of beer afterwards. The concentrated fury of my threshing resembled a whirlwind, an earthquake, or Doomsday. In the zeal and zest of my shepherding, I sometimes drove the animals over the cliff, but I made up for that by folding in wild goats and hares along with the sheep.

'I was a doer, not a thinker in those days, and in the end I fell in love with a woman named Dora, and I could not leave her. So I remained, and when word of it came to the ears of the Faery court they bade me move on. That I did, until my lovely Dora grew old and withered away and died in my arms at last. Then for a long time I was alone in your world and ceased to work at the harvest. In the end the King and Queen took pity on me and let me return. But I was unused to company, even of my own kind by then, and so here I came, to this cave, and here I have lived ever since.'

He fell silent then, and I knew in my heart that these were more words than he had spoken aloud in many years, and that speaking them had meant much to him.

◆ ◆ ◆

Soon after this Kee returned and I took my leave of the Phenoderee. He shook my hand as we parted, and I was reminded that not one of the faeries I had met had ever touched me or allowed me to touch them. This I felt was a measure of the gratitude the Phenoderee felt at my visit, which had somehow brought about a healing within him that had long been needed.

The Faery Rade *

On this night I have taken part in the most wondrous event. It being Midsummer's Eve, I thought it most important that I visit the Lands Beneath – for then, above all other times, there is such a great noise of Faery activity in the Lands Above that I wished to discover more of this.

◆ ◆ ◆

When I arrived at the Great Hall, everything was abuzz with quiet excitement. Seldom have I known the Faery realm so active or so busy. In general, whatever tasks and activities take place there, they are done with such quietness, and so inconspicuously, that there is always an air of peace and quiet. Now I sensed at once that something unusual was about to happen.

Kee came forward almost at once, his eyes shining especially bright, I thought. 'Welcome, Robert Kirk,' he said. 'I am glad you have come to witness the Rade.'

'What is this – Rade?' I asked.

'Why,' said he, 'surely you must know, since your kind speak of it so often. It is when the whole court rides forth into your world.'

* The word seems to have the meaning of both 'ride' and 'raid'. I have therefore left the spelling as Kirk gives it. Ed.

I had indeed heard something to this effect – that on Midsummer night all the Faery were abroad and that wise mortals should stay inside for fear of mischief. I said as much to Kee, whose turn it was to look puzzled.

'Does your kind really see us in that way?' he asked. 'Surely the glory of our coming is a rare thing which must be enjoyed by all!'

'Perhaps so,' said I. 'But do not forget that among the folk of the Lands Above your kind are often seen as fearful beings, daemons with flaming eyes, out to do us harm.'

'That is a cause of sorrow,' said Kee. 'It is to be hoped that when your writings about us are read by your kind, they will think otherwise.'

In my heart I wondered then – as I wonder now – if I will ever show these words to anyone, and doubt even more if they will be understood. But I put such thoughts from me for the time, and asked Kee to tell me more about the Rade.

'The court is even now assembling,' said Kee. 'Soon we shall be ready to depart. This night the Lands Beneath will be almost empty, for most of our kind will go forth. If it is your wish,' he added, 'I will find a steed for you so that you may ride with us.'

A sense of excitement tempered somewhat with trepidation ran through me. I am not all that skilled upon a horse, and guessed that any steed of Faery stock would be far from gentle. None the less, I knew that this was an opportunity that should not be missed, and a great honour also, and so I gave my assent.

The Great Procession

Kee bade me wait and slipped away. Moments later he returned, leading a sturdy brown mare with a gentle eye. Seeing my evident relief, Kee laughed. 'It was in my mind that you would want a human steed. This is no Faery mount, but it will carry you safely tonight.'

Thankfully I took the reins, and at this moment its strange call rang out through the Lands Beneath.

'It is time,' Kee said. 'May you ride well tonight, Robert Kirk. I shall be close at hand.'

He moved away again and I saw a great procession emerging from the Great Hall. First came the Faery King and Queen, splendid in clothes of green and gold, riding upon steeds that were taller and finer than any human animal, richly decorated and sporting many jewels about saddle and bridle.

As they passed, I bowed my head and doffed my hat, as befits royalty, and received a stern but kindly glance by way of acknowledgement. Then the troupe of the Faery races came by. Mostly it was the Sidhe who rode in the van, but behind them came many others, some on foot, others riding steeds so strange that I am wanting the words to describe them. I saw there the Sylvan elves, striding along behind the mounted folk – and even the Kobbold trotted in the rear, seeming to have no difficulty keeping up despite their shortness of stature. Others, seeming at times so insubstantial to my eyes that I could detect no details of their true form, drifted like dandelion seeds on the wind.

Then Kee's voice called to me and, mounting with care on to my gentle steed, I followed the troupe, finding myself in the rear of the Sidhe contingent without quite knowing how I came there.

Kee rode at my side and turned his great eyes upon me. 'Be ready, Robert Kirk,' he said.

Across the Heavens

Before I had time to wonder what it was I should be ready for, I found that we were outside, in my own world, and we were moving far faster than any normal mount could travel. My own placid beast ran with the rest, doubtless touched by Faery magic.

Faster and faster we rode, until the landscape became a blur upon either side. I clutched the reins until my knuckles showed white, and crouched close at the neck of my steed. Then, all at

once, the rhythm of its stride changed and I realized, to my terror,
that we had left the earth and were flying!

I shut my eyes tight, expecting at any moment to come
crashing down to earth. When this did not occur, I very carefully
sat up, opened my eyes and looked around.

What a magnificent sight I beheld! The Faery Rade spread out
across the sky like a trail of stars, or a fiery comet's tail. Around us
the vast expanse of the heavens glowed and glittered, lit by the
great round face of the Midsummer moon.

The cold night air rushed by, plucking at my clothing and
battering against my face. All around, the people of Faery, in
their glorious array, galloped. At times I heard a voice raised in
what I took to be song, though such as human voice could never
give utterance to. A light was around us, such that I thought the
sky must be lit for any mortal who might glance up from the
earth below.

How long we rode I cannot say. Time itself seemed to slow. I fell into a strange state, half dream, half waking, from which I was roused only when I heard Kee speaking my name. With a start I found myself at the entrance to the Faery howe, though how we had come there, or what course we had followed in the Faery Rade, I know not.

'The rest of this night is for our kind alone,' said Kee. 'We are glad that you rode with us this night, Robert Kirk. Go now with our blessing and return when next you wish.'

So my adventure ended. I cannot help but wonder what great and secret sports take place even now in the Lands Beneath! For myself, I shall remember always the ride across the night sky, and can feel only sadness that to others of my kind, far below us, most would have felt only fear or horror at the sight. But if any were bold enough to look more closely, and saw a very mortal man in the midst of the host of Faery, that man was I, Robert Kirk, who went this night on the Faery Rade.

Belief in the Faery Realms

I s it madness to believe, as I now believe, in the existence of the Subterranean realm? Or invisibility, which I myself have experienced? Many would call it so, and others would go further and say that I blaspheme against the Lord God for allowing the existence of such creatures as the Sidhe or the Sylvan elves.

Yet I believe it should not be repugnant to either reason or religion to believe in an invisible world, or a people to us for the most part invisible – people having a commonwealth, laws and economy, made known to us by obscure hints of the few admitted to their converse. It is no more necessary for us to know there are such beings and Subterranean cavern inhabitants than it is necessary to know distinctly the nine orders of angels; or with what oil the lamp of the sun is maintained, so long and so regularly; or why the moon is called a great luminary while it only appears to be so – or if the moon be inhabited – yet surely our lives are enriched by such knowledge?

●●●

If the words I write in this book should ever fall into the hands of wiser men than I and be thought only a fancy and forgery because obscure and for so long unknown to most of mankind, I would list by way of defence the existence of the Antipodes and the inhabitants of America, who though they are as real as ourselves, and very bone of our bone, yet on their first discovery were looked on as people from faery tale, and those who reported them laughed out of court as the inventors of ridiculous Utopias and strange dreams.

But if indeed the things seen by Seers are real, their presages and predictions found to be true, then the truth of all that I have seen seems best explained by a simple fact: that the courteous endeavours of our fellow creatures in the invisible world may be meant to convince us of the existence of a Deity, or of spirits; and of a possible and harmless correspondence between ourselves and the dwellers of the Lands Beneath, even in this life.

So too I understand that their intent in allowing such communication as I have here described is to caution and warn us, to tell us of the orders of beings with bodies of air, condensed and curiously shaped, who live next to man, superior to us in understanding, yet unconfined; and of their life, habitation and influence on man – which may be greater than that of the stars.

This, it seems to me, is a fit knowledge for these last atheistic ages, wherein the profanity of men's lives has debauched and blinded their understanding. Nor does the ceasing of the Seer's visions, upon his migration into foreign lands, make his conjectures any less probable. On the contrary, it confirms greatly my account of an invisible people, guardian over and careful of men, who have their different offices and abilities in distant countries just as much as here. For thus we may see that every country and kingdom has its spirits or powers assisting in government and polity.

A Scottish Seer, banished to America, and being a stranger there – as much to its invisible as to its visible inhabitants – and wanting the familiarity of his former correspondents, may not have the same warnings, visions and predictions which were granted him by unseen companions in his own country. Certainly it is far too great an honour for Scotland to have such seldom-seen watchers and predominant powers over it alone, and all other nations wholly destitute of the like. Yet it seems to me that all people want the key to the box containing the magic of the faeries, and the exact method of correspondence with them, and for myself, or for those like me, who have wandered into the Lands Beneath, to claim this for our own would be a most wicked and selfish act.

A Strange Encounter

I grow more certain that there are two distinct factions within the realm, and that while one is well disposed towards us, the other is not. That this may become a cause of strife between these two groups is also something that I believe to be possible.

Today I saw one that came from the Unseelie court, or, at least, one I believe to be of that faction. At my request, Kee had taken me to a place where I might glimpse a creature deemed rare, even among the Subterranean dwellers: the White Hart. Among mortals it is known to presage wondrous events and is said to have led many of King Arthur's knights to adventure or death. Kee informed me that the creature was rarely sighted in the Lands Beneath, but had been lately reported in a stretch of wild land which I believed to be northwards from the lower gate of the Faery howe. Thither we made our way, as always travelling more swiftly and uncertainly than I could wholly fathom.

'Here we shall catch a sight of the White Beast,' Kee told me, his eyes shining especially brightly. 'It will surely bring great luck.'

'Do you then believe in luck?' I asked, surprised by this remark.

'We believe that some events which happen suggest that things may go well for us, and that others presage more doubtful occurrences. Our world is full of signs and wonders as, surely, is your own.'

Having no good answer to this, and wishing to reflect, I said no more on this topic. We walked in silence for a time, crossing rougher terrain than any I had seen before, though even this possessed a stark beauty of its own.

Great tumbled boulders lay scattered on the ground, which was patterned with a kind of close-growing plant, not unlike heather but not heather as I know it, for I examined it more closely and found it to be quite different in its essential form. Ahead the ground began to rise towards a valley of sorts – though, as ever, I find it hard to recall the exact nature of the place.

Here it was that we found ourselves confronted by a figure that I at first took to be one of the same Sidhe race as my companion, but as we stood before him, I saw that there were subtle differences. Here was the same elfin look, the same narrow face and slanting brows, the same slender stature and gracefulness, but rather than the golden or green eyes of the Sidhe I had so far encountered, I found myself looking into eyes that were, shockingly, red – and though set in a face of great purity showed only cold hostility towards both myself and my companion.

I saw from his demeanour that Kee was not only surprised by this meeting but also somewhat disturbed. I saw his hand stray towards his sword, only to fall from it, as if he regretted the action. The being before us had also noticed the movement and seemed to grow even colder in that moment.

There followed a swift exchange between the two Sidhe, and though I could not understand the words they spoke, yet I felt they were far from friendly. Whatever passed between them was soon over, and the dark Sidhe (for such I thought him, though he dressed in the same light colours as my companion) turned away. As he did so, I felt myself subject to the kind of regard I had not felt since first coming to the Lands Beneath. This time, the scrutiny seemed to me more invasive than before, as though the dark Sidhe probed deeply into my very soul with those strange red eyes. Then he was gone from our sight, folding back, as it seemed, into the landscape in that disconcerting way the Sidhe have. As he did so, I thought I caught a word that seemed to be directed at me: 'Sluagh!'

I found myself unwontedly disturbed by this and looked to my companion for help. 'That fellow seemed ill-disposed towards us.'

Kee looked at me. 'He is from the Unseelie court. They have little time for mortals, nor do they like us over much, though we are cousins. We have ancient quarrels.'

'That word – what was it? – Sluagh. Was he referring to me?'

For the first time I detected something in my companion that I might, in one of my own kind, have deemed embarrassment.

'It is a word used to describe humans who are dead but who refuse to depart. It is a harsh word. I am sorry that you heard

it used in this way of someone who is our guest.'

'It would pain me to be a cause of strife among your people,' I ventured.

'What our King and Queen have ordained should not be questioned,' answered Kee. 'You have been made welcome in our land, and thus you shall remain.' He turned those astonishing green-gold eyes upon me. 'Let us not speak of these things any further.' Then he added, 'It seems we shall not see the White Beast today. Let us return whence we came.'

• • •

This seeming chance encounter has given me much pause for thought. Am I, inadvertently, a cause for enmity between the two courts? I fear this may well be so. If I am right, then possibly I may be able to do something to heal the breach. Yet I remember Kee's words to me, that there were 'old quarrels' between the Seelie and Unseelie courts. I must think more upon these matters.*

* There seems to have been a gap of several weeks between this last entry and the one that follows. We may assume that Kirk was too involved in planning his next journey, an account of which follows, written hurriedly and with none of Kirk's usual careful penmanship. Ed.

The Unseelie Court

I have been where no mortal man should go, and must pay the price. Reviewing all that I have written in this notebook, I am forced to the conclusion that the Subterranean world is preparing for war. None, I feel, would be excluded from this, for the lesser tribes would certainly take sides, some following the Seelie court and others the Unseelie. In my innermost thoughts I have felt somehow responsible – as though my presence in the Lands Beneath had brought to the boil ancient grievances, stirred up old quarrels. For days I agonized over the situation, praying and meditating on what I might do to prevent this terrible rupture. How could I allow a world that has come to mean so much to me, to represent a kind of perfection utterly absent from our own world, to injure itself because of me?

So it was that I decided upon a course of action which now seems to me the product of utter madness. I must visit the Unseelie court myself and do what I could to repair the damage I had unintentionally caused.

As it befell, this was a far easier task than I had imagined. Of late my companion, Kee, has been more often absent – another factor in my belief that the Lands Beneath were preparing for conflict – though perhaps it was no more than an increased measure of trust that left me to wander ever more freely in the Subterranean realm in the belief that I would not overstep the bounds that had been agreed upon when I first entered the Lands Beneath.

I made a point to revisit several places shown to me earlier. I spent some time studying and sketching the plants which I had glimpsed on my first visit to the Sylvan elves.* Thus I became so familiar a sight that I was, to all intents, ignored.

So the day dawned when I was prepared to take my chance. I had learned enough of the geography of the Lands Beneath, such as it existed at all, to know that to reach any part of the Subterranean realm was as much a matter of will as of physical effort. None the less, I began by making my way, as far as I could tell in that subtly changing landscape, to that place where Kee and I had encountered the dark Sidhe. I suppose I believed that in so doing I might be closer to the Unseelie court, though its actual location was unknown to me.

In the end, it was all too easy. I simply willed myself to stand again at the entrance to the valley where Kee and I had gone to see the White Hart. Once there I concentrated with all my intellectual powers on the idea of the dark Sidhe and of what I imagine the Unseelie court might look like. As I did so there appeared before me a door of sorts – though in fact it was no more than a frame, for upon looking through it I saw but the same landscape in which I already stood. By now I had spent enough time in the Lands Beneath to know that such confusion to my eyes was but an illusion. Therefore I stepped boldly up to the door and, taking a deep breath, walked though.

* Sadly these sketches have never been found, if indeed they survived the events that followed. Ed.

The Dark Court

At once I found myself in a dimly lit place, not at all like the open and brightly lit halls of the Seelie court. Even now I am at a loss to describe it with any firm definition, except to say that if the court of the Faery King and Queen to which I had first been ushered on entering the Faery howe was lit by the sun, then this place in which I now stood was under the sway of the moon. Everywhere shadows clustered thickly, as though draped from the roof (if roof there truly was) of the Subterranean realm. Yet the place was not wholly dark, for globes of pearly luminescence floated in the air like bubbles of light.

By this strange and altogether unearthly glow, I saw a path snaking away before me. Hesitatingly, I glanced behind, expecting to see the door and the bright lands beyond. But to my dismay they were no longer there – only still more of the strange haunted landscape that now surrounded me upon every side. Having little or no choice in the matter, I elected to follow the path before me, noticing that the ground upon either side seemed oddly bleached and dry, as though the lack of true light (why I should deem it true or otherwise I am at a loss to say) had left the place somehow starved.

It was hard to see any distance on either hand or behind, and though my eyes quickly adjusted to the strange pearly glow, it was most like walking in a mist of the kind that often descends upon an evening traveller in the Lands Above.

◆ ◆ ◆

Since time has so little meaning in the Subterranean realm I cannot say for how long I walked. It seemed to be some while, perhaps as much as an hour, but as ever I had little or no sense of distance by which to judge my progress. However, I began to be aware of what I can only describe as a thickening of the air before me, until out of the gloom arose the walls of a building.

If such a structure could be said to frown, then this is the term that best describes the Unseelie court. Something about its very architecture spoke of heaviness and intensity. I could not help but contrast this with the Seelie court, all open to the light and full of music and dancing. Here, I felt, no one had truly danced for millennia.

How much of this, or indeed of what followed, should be seen as subjective I cannot, in all honesty, say. Was I determined to prejudge the Unseelie court? Did my encounter with the dark Sidhe dispose me to look upon the home of such beings as somehow the opposite of the realm of light occupied by my friends? I cannot deny that such thoughts may well have coloured my experiences — so subtle are the Faery realms that, as I now believe, my conscious fear and negativity may well have been enhanced by the place, or may equally well have influenced all that I saw.

Be that as it may, as I made my way towards the Unseelie court there arose before me an entrance that seemed rather carved from the bones of the earth than constructed by any hand. All sharp edges and planes, as though whoever had been responsible for its creation had intended it to be forbidding and unfriendly.

With my heart in my mouth, I stepped through this fearsome entrance and found myself in a hall of truly vast proportions, made even more daunting by the fact that much of its floor, walls and the great forest of pillars that lined it upon all sides had been polished until they shone, giving back echo upon echo of the pale light emitted by countless floating globes.

The effect was of black marble, yet on closer examination I saw that whatever stone had been used it was something I could not recognize. It was as though the Unseelie court had been fashioned from something wholly other, perhaps as a sign to all of its separateness from the rest of the Lands Beneath.

At first I thought the place empty, then I became aware of a curious rustling sound that seemed to come from everywhere and nowhere in that vast hall. With this awareness I began to notice the shapes that moved hither and yon among the forest of pillars. With this awareness I sensed that the beings thronging that place were suddenly aware of my presence also, and then at once I found myself surrounded by tall slender beings, each one like my own familiar friends in appearance, except that the cast of their faces was stern, and devoid of gentleness, and that their eyes burned red in their pale faces.

I realize upon reflection that none actually touched me. I was simply hemmed in and forced to move in the direction required by the presence of so many. It was as though they were possessed of a kind of aura which exerted a force upon me, so that without my feeling even the littlest touch, I was compelled to walk forward through the Great Hall until I stood at last before two thrones.

• • •

Here I must pause for a moment, in order to speak of something I am still unable to explain. In almost every way, the Unseelie court mirrored that of the Seelie. The same space, the same two seats, even the mighty beings who occupied them, seemed, as it were, reflections of the King and Queen of Faery whom I had encountered on my first visit. Yet all were different. This is something that I now see must lie at the heart of the Lands Beneath. Kee had mentioned to me the division that existed between the courts, and even the Faery King himself had spoken of this originally. Can it be that on some distant day, who knows how many ages ago, the oldest dwellers within the Subterranean realm had consciously chosen to go their own way and had, as a result, developed along similar yet wholly different lines? I cannot speak of this more, and I may have little time to complete this account, but I leave it for others to judge whether this is so or not.

Facing the Unseelie Court

So I stood before the King and Queen of the Unseelie court, wishing that I had not been so foolish as to come there, and wondering what I had hoped to achieve. It was the King who bent his gaze upon me, and in that moment I felt that I was naked to my soul before him.

'What do you want here, sluagh?' he demanded.

His voice, as I heard it, was lower in timbre than that of my friends of the Sidhe, but just as beautiful to hear. Indeed, for all its dark and forbidding nature, everything about the Unseelie court was in every way as lovely as that of the Seelie – save that this beauty seemed more perilous, as though to look upon it for too long might bring about some deeper change within those who saw it.

Forcing myself to look up at the two great Faery monarchs, and wishing to be as direct as I might be, I stammered out the words that came to me. 'I am concerned that the courts of Faery may be preparing for war, and that I may be the cause of it.'

A murmur ran through the concourse of the dark Sidhe, like the wind in a field of corn. I heard the word 'sluagh' on many lips, but also other words which, by their intonation, I took to be expressions of surprise.

The Unseelie King, however, was unmoved. His voice betrayed no emotion and his strange red eyes regarded me as he might a creature of inconceivable minority.

'It is true that we object to the presence of your kind in our world,' he said at last. 'But this is an ancient quarrel between

ourselves and our brethren of the white court. You have
gone even further by entering where
no creature such as you may ever
come. Do you truly imagine that by
doing so you can set matters right?'

'I wish only to put right any
damage I may have done to the Lands
Beneath,' I answered. 'If by my presence
I have offended you, I would do all in
my power to make things good.'

Silence greeted my speech, and in
that moment I had time to reflect upon
words spoken so hastily, as it seemed. Yet
I was sincere in my wish to avert what
seemed so real a danger and felt I had
done what must be done.

For the first time the Queen looked
towards me. I was struck again by the
likeness between her and the Seelie
Queen, who had so kindly welcomed me
on my first visit to the Faery howe. Her
voice also reminded me so much of the
other Queen that I wondered again if
they might not be sisters.

'You have trespassed where none of your
kind may come. The punishment for this is
death. What have you to say in reply?'

A shudder passed over me at this and once again
I wished myself anywhere but in that place. Yet I
could not now back down, or else my journey was
without meaning.

'If that is the punishment I must endure, then
endure it I shall,' I said as steadily as I might.

Now I felt the regard of both monarchs, while
again a ripple of sound passed through the ranks of the Unseelie
court. At the same moment there came another sound, like the
ringing of a small, high-toned bell, and there at my side stood Kee.
His bright face seemed to shine even more intensely in that dark
place, and I saw that those of the Unseelie court who stood nearest
drew back, and that some even shaded their eyes.

Waiting for Judgement

Despite his unannounced appearance, Kee bowed low before
the King and Queen, and only when he received a sign to
stand up did he do so. He then began to speak rapidly.

How the conversation went I could not say, since I could follow
none of it, but in a while Kee bowed again to the Unseelie King
and Queen and then, turning to me, said, 'We may depart now.'

'But,' said I, 'am I not under sentence of death?'

'So you remain, for breaking the most sacred of our laws,' he
said sternly. 'But the Lords of the Unseelie court have not the
power to condemn you solely, without the agreement of my own

King and Queen. These matters will be discussed in my court this night. For the present you are commanded to remain in the realm until such time as this matter is resolved.'

With these words I found myself, with such a sudden and abrupt transposition that my head spun with it, back at the gates of the Seelie court. Here I was instructed to wait. I sat, watching as an increasingly large number of the Sidhe, and representatives of the other races, entered the Great Hall. Normally, I would have taken the opportunity to observe these beings, several of whom I had not seen before, but I was deeply shaken by the events of the day, and now more than ever wondered at the wisdom of my actions.

The Judgement of the Seelie Court

Time passed in the way all time passes in the Lands Beneath – drop by drop, and with no real sense of its movement. The light remained bright in the dome of heaven, and a small wind stirred the leaves of the clusters of flowers, the names and natures of which I had so lately enquired after, that grew by the gates of the hall. And now again I breathed in the magical and calming perfume they emitted. Beyond this, a strange hush fell over the

Faery realm. More than at any time before, during my visits below, I felt a pressure of events happening with a gravity that was normally foreign to that merry world.

• • •

In time Kee appeared at the entrance to the hall and beckoned me to follow him. I entered the lofty place and found there the greatest gathering of the Faery races that I had seen in all my journeys to the Subterranean world. The King and Queen sat as ever upon their crystal thrones, but this time it was the King who spoke to me.

'Robert Kirk, you have broken the laws by which our world is governed, of which you were well advised. You have entered where it is forbidden to mortal man to go. What have you to say for yourself?'

'Sir, madam,' said I, 'I meant no harm. Do not think it for a moment. I have been deeply honoured by the gift of being permitted access to your world.

Indeed, I have come to look upon it as a place that is dear to me. It was purely because of my fear that my presence here was about to throw your realm into strife that I entered where I was forbidden – hoping, as I did, that I might prevent further trouble.'

'Yet instead you have brought greater strife upon us all,' said the King. 'The Lords of the Unseelie court have every right to demand your life. What do you say to this?'

'As I have already spoken, so do I say again. If my life will help prevent the spilling of Faery blood, then I will give it up, and that right gladly.'

Silence followed this, and it was the voice of the Faery Queen I heard next. As she had done on the day when I first entered the Lands Beneath, she spoke gently to me.

'We honour your courage and your concern, Robert Kirk. Few of your kind would be willing to give up the brief span of their years for our sake. Because of this we will offer you a way to redeem your actions, and to put an end to this quarrel between our two courts.'

She paused for a moment, and I found the courage to look up into that beautiful, remote face. No smile or least touch of warmth touched the Faery Queen's fathomless eyes, and her voice was as cool and clear as crystal as she spoke above me so that the whole court might hear.

'This is our judgment: that you, Robert Kirk, of the Lands Above, must choose either to lose your life, as the Unseelie court demands, or to remain here for the rest of your days, never more to look upon or return to the Lands Above, upon pain of losing your life. Do you agree to this, and how do you choose?'

In that moment, time truly seemed to come to a halt. Even in that place where hours and minutes have no meaning, I felt that my whole life had come to a stop, just as surely as if I had already accepted death. My first thought was for my family – never to see them again seemed such a terrible thing that I felt tears start in my eyes at the very thought of it. Yet the alternative was just as much of an ending, and who knew whether there might not come a day when changes in the Lands Beneath might one day permit me to go home?

As I stood in thought for that moment, I felt suddenly the weight of the bag at my shoulder, all but forgotten in the tension of the moment, in which this book, together with my sketching materials, lay. They came to my mind then, a final gleam of hope. I looked up at the Faery King and Queen.

'Sir and madam,' I said, 'if I might have leave to ask one thing of you, then I will gladly assent to your judgement.'

The Lord and Lady of the Seelie court bowed their heads in acknowledgement.

'Give me leave to return home one last time, to set my affairs in order and to take leave of my family. I give you my word that I will return hither on the morrow, and afterwards I shall remain here until such time, if ever, as your majesties might wish to set me free.'

'It shall be as you wish, Robert Kirk,' said the Queen at once. 'See to it that you keep your word to us.'

A Great Adventure

Thus I was dismissed, and made my way by the road I now knew so well back to the entrance of the Faery howe, coming forth but a moment later than I had entered there, still under a bright moon. There, as I breathed in the familiar sense of the world I had known all my life until but lately, I realized that it is the eve of Midsummer, a fitting time, it seems, to join the Faery court.

I made my way slowly back to this grey stone house where I have spent many happy days in the Lands Above. Here my dear son Colin, who has lately returned to live with me, sleeps still. I shall not wake him. Instead I shall write a letter to him, and leave behind this book, as a testimony to my work and to the end of my time in this world. I pray to my God and Saviour to keep him safe, and if it be His will to preserve the soul of his faithful servant on earth, Robert Kirk, safe from harm in time to come.

I do not know if I shall ever come forth from the Faery realms again, or ever look upon the faces of those I love, but in my heart I know that I shall see them again when the Good Lord takes us all into His care. For the moment, I shall end this account, being a faithful record of my journeys to the Lands Beneath. Though my heart is heavy to turn my back upon this world, yet I would be false if I did not record that this is the beginning of a great adventure, and that I shall take fresh paper and pens with me, with which I may continue this record as long as I am permitted to do so.

Ended this twenty-first day of June in the year of Our Lord, sixteen hundred and ninety-two.

A Letter from Robert Kirk to his Son, Colin

The following letter came to light among the papers in the collection of Mrs Jean Seldy of Balquhidder. It had evidently become separated from the rest of the manuscript and was not discovered until I was already most of the way through the process of editing the text presented here. The letter reproduced here moved me greatly, and seemed to be a fitting coda to the story of Robert Kirk. Bearing in mind the writer's hope that his account might one day see the light of day as a published book, I am glad to have achieved this in his name, as his son evidently failed to do.

The Rectory, Aberfoyle
21st June 1692

My Very Dear Son,

The sky is stained bright gold by the setting of the Midsummer sun as I write these words to you. I am soon to depart upon a journey from which I may not easily return, and it is my dearest wish that you should know something of the events that have led me to this point in my life, and to the wonderful tidings that my journeys into that place that men refer to as the Faery realm have brought me.

Many will think me mad to write of these things, and declare that my claims are false and the result of delusions. I must beg you to believe me when I say that

every word I write here is true, and that you, my
dearest son, are the only living soul to whom I have
felt able to entrust these
revelations. Your dear mother,
God rest her soul, would have
understood, though sadly she
is no more.

You will be aware that I
have studied the mystery of
the Faery races for many years
now, and that I had fervent
hope that the notes I have kept
would one day see the light of
day in the form of a book. This
seems now unlikely to happen,
and it is indeed unlikely that
any man or woman now living would wish to read
what I have to tell. Yet someone must hear me, and
therefore I have chosen to entrust these matters to you,
in the hope that you may be moved to believe, and
that you may also forgive me for what may seem a
betrayal of my role as a minister of God's holy word.
Yet it has always been my intent to strengthen the
work of the Lord here on earth by a study of these
things. It should not, surely, be considered repugnant to
reason that an invisible realm, peopled by those not
normally available to ordinary sight, should exist, and
that they should furthermore possess a commonwealth
with laws, economy and ways of their own. It is no
more needful for us to have proof of the existence of
such beings than it is for us to see angels with our own
eyes, since in both we may choose to believe.

Thus, my dear son, I have written of my visits to the Lands Beneath us, which I believe none the less to be part of God's Holy Creation. And I have told, in words and pictures, what I have seen there, so that those who seek to know the truth may see it writ large. Believe me or believe me not, I do but write of what these poor eyes of mine have witnessed almost daily over these past few years.

Soon it will be time for me to return to the Subterranean realm, as I have promised to do in return for being permitted to walk abroad once more briefly in the land of men. When I am gone, this record must stand as a testimony to my work. I beg you, therefore, my dear son, to see that this book is preserved for others to read.

I am, on this twenty-first day of June in the Year of Our Lord sixteen hundred and ninety-two, and ever thereafter,

Your devoted and loving father,

Robert Kirk

Afterword: The Disappearance of the Rev. Robert Kirk

The mystery surrounding Robert Kirk's death, or perhaps one should say disappearance, is one of the great curiosities of folklore and history. Several accounts of the events that took place in 1692 and after still exist, and I feel it important to include some record of them here, since, especially in the light of Kirk's extraordinary claims, they seem more than a little relevant.

According to the words of one Patrick Graham, writing some time after the events, Kirk was taking the air in his nightshirt on the night of 21 June 1692, on 'a certain fairy hill close to his home', when he collapsed. His body was carried home and a doctor called. He was pronounced dead that evening, and with a great deal of sorrow and morning his body was interred in Aberfoyle churchyard. The inscription on the tomb, which may still be seen to this day, reads as follows:

HIC SEPULTUS

ILLE EVANGELII

PROMULGATOR

ACCURATUS

ET

LINGUAE HIBERNIAE

LUMEN

M. ROBERTUS KIRK

ABERFOILE PASTOR

OBIT 21 JUNE 1692

AETAT 48

But this is far from being the end of the story. According to Mr Graham, who was a collateral descendant of Kirk's, the ghost of the dead minister appeared to one of his relations (who, we are not told) and gave a message intended for a cousin – one Graham of Duchray. The message was to this effect: that Kirk was not dead but the captive of Faeryland. He then declared that he would return at the christening of his cousin's child, and that if the man could throw a knife over the apparition, he might thus be released.

The christening duly took place and there, sure enough, Kirk's 'ghost' appeared. So astonished was Graham of Duchray that he forgot to throw the knife – presumably a reference to the Faery fear of iron – and with a cry the vision departed, never to be seen again.

However, the strange story of Robert Kirk's incarceration in the Faery world never entirely died out. The great folklorist W. Y. Evans-Wentz found it still flourishing in Aberfoyle more than 200 years later. There the woman who kept the keys to the church told him that Kirk's tomb contained a coffin full simply of stones. Kirk himself, she said, had gone into the Faery howe, which she pointed out to Evans-Wentz, and was never seen again.

More astonishing still, and true testimony to the power of such stories, the folklorist Katharine Briggs, author of numerous books on Faery traditions, heard a variation of the same story as recently as 1943. Visiting a friend, she met a young woman who had recently rented the old manse at Aberfoyle – the house in which Kirk had composed his account of the Lands Beneath. It seems that the young woman had been about to give birth, and that she had wished particularly to get home to the manse in time for the event to take place there. For, as she said, the local people had told her that if a first child was born and christened there, and if the mother was to stick a knife into a particular chair believed to have belonged to the good reverend, then he would at last be released from captivity.

It seems that the belief continues still that Kirk may yet be alive in the timeless realm, and may one day be set free. Of course, this is something to which no contemporary student of folklore would give credence. However, the undoubted power of the Reverend Robert Kirk's words, particularly as they are now finally revealed, certainly do give one pause for thought.

JOHN MATTHEWS
OXFORD, 2004

Further Reading

There have been two editions of Robert Kirk's *Secret Commonwealth* in recent years. Both include important commentaries on Kirk and his writing. They represent the manuscript versions currently held by the National Library of Scotland and the Edinburgh University Library. This last named also holds some of Kirk's notebooks, though not those printed here.

The Secret Commonwealth, by Robert Kirk, edited with commentary by Stewart Sanderson (D. S. Brewer Ltd, Cambridge, 1976)

Robert Kirk, Walker between Worlds: A New Edition of 'The Secret Commonwealth of Elves, Fauns and Fairies', by R. J. Stewart (Element Books Ltd, Shaftesbury, Dorset, 1990)

The following brief list includes some of the most important and readily available books on the subject of Faery beliefs and traditions.

Briggs, Katharine, *Dictionary of Fairies* (Allen Lane, London, 1976)

Evans-Wentz, W. Y., *Fairy Faith in Celtic Countries* (Lemma Publishing Corp., New York, 1973)

Franklin, Anna, *The Illustrated Encyclopaedia of Fairies* (Vega, London, 2002)

Henderson, Lizanne and Edward J. Cowan, *Scottish Fairy Belief* (Tuckwell Press, East Lothian, 2001)

Keightly, Thomas, *Fairy Mythology* (Wildwood House, London, 1981)

Matthews, John, *The Sidhe: Wisdom from the Celtic Otherworld* (Lorian Association, Issaquah, WA, 2004)

Matthews, John and Caitlín, *A Fairy Tale Reader* (HarperCollins, London, 1991)

Narvaez, Peter (ed.), *The Good People* (University Press of Kentucky, Lexington, 1991)

Spence, Lewis, *British Fairy Origins* (Aquarian Press, Wellingborough, 1981)

Stewart, R. J., *The Living World of Faery* (Gothic Image Publications, Glastonbury, 1995)

Index

Acknowledgements

Executive Editor Brenda Rosen
Managing Editor Clare Churly
Editor Lesley Levene
Executive Art Editor Sally Bond
Designer Pia Ingham for Cobalt Id
Illustrators George Sharp, Rob McCaig
Production Manager Louise Hall